In memory of
Burl C. and Joseph C.
Two men that believed in being of service to others and carrying the message of recovery to the still sick and suffering addict.

John R.

Table of Contents

WE MADE DIRECT AMENDS TO SUCH PEOPLE WHEREVER POSSIBLE, EXCEPT WHEN TO DO SO WOULD INJURE THEM OR OTHERS

STEP TEN

WE CONTINUED TO TAKE PERSONAL INVENTORY AND WHEN WE WERE WRONG PROMPTLY ADMITTED IT

STEP ELEVEN

WE SOUGHT THROUGH PRAYER AND MEDITATION TO IMPROVE OUR CONSCIOUS CONTACT WITH GOD AS WE UNDERSTOOD HIM, PRAYING ONLY FOR KNOWLEDGE OF HIS WILL FOR US AND THE POWER TO CARRY THAT OUT

STEP TWELVE

HAVING HAD A SPIRITUAL AWAKENING AS A RESULT OF THESE STEPS, WE TRIED TO CARRY THIS MESSAGE TO ADDICTS, AND TO PRACTICE THESE PRINCIPLES IN ALL OUR AFFAIRS

THE PRINCIPLES OF RECOVERY

STEP ONE

We Admitted We Were Powerless Over Our Addiction and, That Our Lives Had Become Unmanageable

As a group, we have all come together to support each other in our journey towards addiction recovery. And Step One is where it all begins - by admitting that we are powerless over our addiction and that our lives have become unmanageable.

This step may seem daunting at first, but it is the foundation upon which we build our path towards recovery. To truly understand what this step means, it's important to recognize addiction as a disease - one that affects not only the person struggling with it, but also their loved ones and those around them.

By acknowledging our powerlessness over this disease and recognizing the negative consequences it has had on our lives, we can begin to break through denial and accept help. This is where true healing begins.

Understanding Addiction as a Disease

We can't control our addiction and it's causing chaos in our lives. At first, we might have thought that our substance abuse was a choice or a lack of willpower. However, understanding addiction as a disease has allowed us to see that this is not the case.

Addiction alters the brain's chemistry and causes changes in behavior that are beyond our control. As we continue to use drugs or alcohol, our brains become accustomed to the effects of these substances. Eventually, we need more and more of them just to feel normal. This is called tolerance, and it's one of the defining features of addiction.

We may try to stop using on our own, but withdrawal symptoms and intense cravings make it nearly impossible without help. Admitting that we are powerless over our addiction doesn't mean that we're giving up or resigning ourselves to a life of substance abuse. Rather, it's the first step in taking back control over our lives.

By acknowledging that we cannot overcome addiction on our own, we open ourselves up to seeking treatment and support from others who understand what we're going through. In short, understanding addiction as a disease helps us see that there is hope for recovery. We don't have to struggle alone anymore - there are resources available that can help us reclaim our lives from the grip of addiction.

By admitting powerlessness over this disease, we take an important step towards healing and growth in all areas of life.

The Importance of Acknowledging Powerlessness

You need to acknowledge your powerlessness over addiction in order to begin the journey towards recovery and a manageable life. This is the first step of the 12-step program for addiction recovery, and it's crucial because it helps us understand that we cannot overcome our addiction through our own willpower alone.

We must admit that we are powerless over drugs or alcohol, and that our lives have become unmanageable as a result. Acknowledging powerlessness isn't easy. It can be scary to admit that you don't have control over something that has such a strong hold on your life. However, this admission is necessary for true healing to take place.

Once we accept our powerlessness, we can begin to seek help from others who have gone through similar struggles and found ways to manage their addiction. It's important to remember that acknowledging powerlessness doesn't mean giving up hope. On the contrary, it's a hopeful step towards recovery because it opens up new possibilities for us.

By admitting that we can't do this alone, we allow ourselves to be vulnerable enough to ask for help from others who understand what we're going through. Acknowledging powerlessness is a critical first step in overcoming addiction. It allows us to recognize our need for support and guidance from others who have walked the same path before us.

While it may feel uncomfortable at first, embracing our vulnerability with honesty and humility sets us on the path towards finding lasting freedom from addiction and living a more manageable life.

Recognizing the Negative Consequences of Addiction

Recognizing the negative consequences of addiction is a crucial step towards understanding the impact it has on our lives. Addiction can lead to a host of problems, such as financial difficulties, strained relationships, and health issues. It's important to acknowledge these consequences in order to fully comprehend the severity of our addiction and its effects on ourselves and those around us.

Financial difficulties are one of the most common negative consequences of addiction. When we're addicted, we may spend money recklessly on drugs or alcohol without considering the long-term ramifications. This can lead to debt, bankruptcy, and even loss of employment if our addiction interferes with work responsibilities.

Strained relationships are another common consequence of addiction. Our loved ones may become frustrated with us for neglecting our responsibilities or prioritizing our addiction over them. We may also find ourselves distancing from friends and family members who don't understand or support our struggles with addiction.

Health issues are perhaps one of the most serious consequences of addiction. Substance abuse can cause both physical and mental health problems that can have lasting effects even after we achieve sobriety. These issues can include organ damage, depression, anxiety disorders, and more.

Recognizing the negative consequences of addiction is essential for gaining a full understanding of how it affects every area of our lives. By acknowledging these consequences - financial difficulties, strained relationships, and health issues - we become more aware of why we need to seek help for our addictions in order to live happier and healthier lives free from substance abuse.

Breaking through Denial and Accepting Help

Breaking through denial can be difficult, but accepting help is a necessary step towards recovery and regaining control of your life's direction. When we're in the grips of addiction, it can be easy to ignore the negative consequences that our actions have on ourselves and those around us.

We might brush off concerns from loved ones or convince ourselves that our behavior isn't as bad as they make it out to be. However, breaking through this denial is crucial if we want to move forward.

To begin with, we must recognize that addiction isn't something we can control on our own. Our willpower may seem strong at first, but eventually, we'll find ourselves slipping back into old habits without proper support. It takes courage to admit that we need help, but doing so opens up a world of opportunities for us.

With the right resources and guidance, we can learn how to manage our cravings and avoid triggers while also addressing any underlying mental health issues.

Once we've accepted help, it's important to stay committed to the recovery process. This means actively participating in support groups or therapy sessions and being honest about our struggles along the way.

Recovery isn't a linear path; there will be setbacks and challenges along the way. However, staying connected with others who understand what we're going through can provide us with much-needed encouragement during difficult times.

Breaking through denial and accepting help may seem daunting at first, but it's an essential step towards overcoming addiction. By recognizing that addiction has made our lives unmanageable and seeking out support from others who have been in similar situations before us, we open up doors to new possibilities for living a fulfilling life free from substance abuse.

Remember: you're never alone in this journey towards recovery!

Embracing the Support of a Recovery Program

By embracing the support of a recovery program, we can begin to build a strong foundation for lasting sobriety and find a community of people who understand our struggles. It takes courage to admit that we need help and open ourselves up to others, but it's an essential step in our journey towards recovery.

A recovery program provides us with the tools and resources necessary to achieve long-term sobriety and improve our overall quality of life. The support of a recovery program can come in many forms, including group therapy sessions, individual counseling, and 12-step programs like Alcoholics Anonymous or Narcotics Anonymous. These programs provide us with the opportunity to connect with others who have faced similar challenges and share their experiences while receiving guidance from trained professionals.

By participating in these programs regularly, we can develop new coping skills, learn healthier ways of dealing with stressors in our lives, and gain valuable insights into addiction and its impact on our lives. In addition to providing us with practical tools for managing addiction, a recovery program also offers emotional support during difficult times.

We may encounter setbacks or face challenges that make it tempting to return to old habits; however, having a supportive community behind us can provide the motivation needed to stay on track towards lasting sobriety. The bonds formed through shared experiences can be incredibly powerful and help us feel less alone as we navigate the ups and downs of recovery.

Ultimately, by embracing the support of a recovery program, we give ourselves the best chance at achieving lasting sobriety. We don't have to go through this journey alone; there are people out there who want nothing more than to see us succeed in overcoming addiction. By taking advantage of these resources and building relationships within these communities, we begin paving the way toward not only healing ourselves but also serving as an inspiration for others who are struggling with their own battles against addiction.

Finding Strength in Unity with Others

You can find strength in unity with others by attending group meetings and connecting with people who understand your struggles.

For example, imagine feeling isolated and alone in your addiction until you attend your first NA meeting and hear the stories of others who have overcome similar challenges, giving you hope for your own recovery journey.

By being part of a community that supports and uplifts each other, you no longer have to face addiction on your own. Attending group meetings also gives you the opportunity to take responsibility for your own actions by sharing your experiences with others.

You can learn from their successes as well as their failure, which helps you gain a better understanding of yourself and what triggers your addictive behavior. This newfound awareness enables you to make healthier choices and break free from negative patterns.

Being part of a recovery program means having access to resources that can help rebuild relationships damaged by addiction. Through support groups, counseling sessions, or sober living homes, you can connect with people who share similar goals for sobriety while receiving guidance from professionals trained in helping addicts recover.

These resources provide a safe space where individuals can come together and offer each other encouragement along the path towards healing. Finding strength in unity is one of the most powerful tools available to those struggling with addiction.

By surrounding yourself with people who are committed to serving others and bettering themselves, you not only get the support needed for personal growth but also contribute positively to the lives of those around you. So take that first step towards recovery today - reach out to a support group or counselor near you!

Addressing the Underlying Issues of Addiction

Addressing the underlying issues of addiction involves identifying and understanding the root causes of addictive behavior in order to develop effective strategies for long-term recovery. Addiction is often a symptom of deeper emotional, psychological, or social issues that have gone unaddressed.

By taking the time to explore and address these underlying issues, we can begin to heal from our addiction and create a more fulfilling life. One common underlying issue of addiction is trauma. Traumatic experiences such as abuse, neglect, or sudden loss can leave us feeling overwhelmed and unable to cope with difficult emotions.

Turning to drugs or alcohol may provide temporary relief from these feelings, but ultimately only compounds the problem. In recovery, it's important to work through this trauma with a qualified therapist or support group in order to develop healthy coping mechanisms.

Another common issue is mental health disorders such as depression, anxiety, bipolar disorder, or ADHD. These conditions can make it difficult for individuals to regulate their emotions and manage daily stressors without turning to substances for relief. Seeking out professional help such as therapy or medication management can be an important component in managing both mental health symptoms and addiction.

Social factors also play a role in addiction. Studies show that people who lack social support are more likely to struggle with addiction than those who have strong relationships with family and friends. Building healthy relationships is essential in recovery; not only do they provide positive reinforcement but they also offer accountability when things get tough.

Ultimately addressing the underlying issues of addiction requires honesty about our own personal struggles and a willingness to seek out help from others who have been there before us. We must be willing to confront uncomfortable truths about ourselves in order to move forward towards lasting change. But by doing so, we not only heal ourselves but also become better equipped to serve others on their journey towards recovery too!

Developing a Strong Foundation for Recovery

Developing a solid foundation for recovery requires taking the time to focus on yourself and your own needs, in order to build a life that is fulfilling and sustainable without substances. It's important to remember that addiction isn't just about using drugs or alcohol; it's often a symptom of deeper issues, such as trauma, anxiety, or depression. To truly recover from addiction, we must address these underlying issues and work towards healing ourselves holistically.

Here are four ways you can start building a strong foundation for recovery:

- Prioritize self-care: This means taking care of your physical, emotional, and spiritual needs. Eat healthy foods, exercise regularly, and practice mindfulness or meditation to reduce stress levels.
- Build a support system: Surround yourself with people who love and support you. Attend 12-step meetings or group therapy sessions where you can connect with others who understand what you're going through.
- Set goals: Having something to work towards can give us purpose and motivation. Set small goals for yourself each day or week–whether it's finishing a project at work or trying a new hobby–and celebrate your accomplishments along the way.
- Practice gratitude: Focusing on what we're grateful for can help shift our perspective away from negative thoughts. Each day, write down three things you're thankful for–even if they seem small.

Remember that building a strong foundation for recovery takes time–but it's worth it in the end. By prioritizing self-care, building a support system, setting goals, and practicing gratitude daily, we can create a fulfilling life without relying on substances. And by doing so, we'll be better equipped to serve others in our community who may be struggling with addiction themselves.

Maintaining Progress and Avoiding Relapse

Maintaining progress and avoiding relapse requires consistent effort and a willingness to confront challenges head-on. One of the most important things we can do is to stay connected with our support network. This includes attending meetings, reaching out to sponsors, and finding ways to give back to others in recovery.

When we isolate ourselves, we become vulnerable to old habits and negative thinking patterns. Another critical aspect of maintaining progress is self-care. This means taking care of our physical, emotional, and spiritual well-being. We need to make time for exercise, healthy eating habits, relaxation techniques such as meditation or yoga, and engaging in activities that bring us joy.

Neglecting these areas can lead us down a slippery slope towards relapse.

It's also crucial to recognize triggers that may lead us back into addictive behaviors. These might include stressors like work or relationship issues, social situations where drugs or alcohol are present, or even certain hours of the day when cravings tend to be strongest. By identifying these triggers early on and developing coping strategies for dealing with them proactively, we can avoid falling back into old patterns.

It's essential not to get complacent in our recovery journey. Addiction is a chronic disease that requires ongoing management and attention. Even after years of sobriety, we must remain vigilant against potential relapse triggers while continuing to grow spiritually and emotionally through service work and personal development efforts.

In summary, maintaining progress in recovery requires constant effort but is well worth it for the benefits gained through sobriety. Through staying connected with our support network, practicing self-care techniques regularly while being mindful of potential triggers that could lead us astray from the path towards healthiness - ultimately leading towards a life filled with happiness!

The Ongoing Journey of Addiction Recovery

Oh boy, here we go again - the ongoing journey of addiction recovery is a wild ride full of ups and downs that no one ever really prepares you for. It's a constant struggle to stay sober and avoid relapse, but it's also a journey of self-discovery and growth.

We learn so much about ourselves during this process, including our triggers, weaknesses, and strengths. One thing that I've learned in my own journey of addiction recovery is that it's not enough to just stay clean or sober. Recovery is an ongoing process that requires us to constantly work on ourselves and our relationships with others.

This means being honest with ourselves when we make mistakes, learning from those mistakes, and making amends whenever possible. At times, the journey can be overwhelming and exhausting. We may feel like giving up or going back to our old ways.

But it's important to remember why we started this journey in the first place - for our own well-being and for the sake of those who love us. It's also helpful to surround ourselves with a supportive community of people who understand what we're going through. The ongoing journey of addiction recovery is not easy, but it's worth it.

It requires honesty, hard work, perseverance, and a willingness to grow as individuals. With time and effort, we can continue down this path towards healing and wholeness - one step at a time.

Frequently Asked Questions

What is the history of the Step One process in addiction recovery programs?

Step One in addiction recovery programs involve admitting powerlessness over addiction and unmanageability of life. It's a crucial first step towards healing and self-awareness. This process has evolved over time, but remains a cornerstone for many seeking recovery.

How can family members and loved ones support someone going through the Step One process?

Supporting a loved one in Step One is like being a trusted guide through a dark forest. Listen without judgment, offer encouragement and resources, and celebrate each step forward in their journey towards recovery.

What are some common misconceptions about Step One and the recovery process?

Don't let misconceptions hold you back from supporting a loved one in recovery. Step One requires admitting powerlessness and unmanageability, but it's not about weakness. It's the first step towards freedom.

How do different types of addiction (e.g. substance abuse, gambling, etc.) affect the Step One process?

Different types of addiction affect the step one process differently. My friend struggled with gambling and it took him longer to admit powerlessness because he thought he could control his behavior. Accepting powerlessness can be difficult, but it's the first step towards recovery.

How does spirituality play a role in the Step One process and addiction recovery?

Spirituality is a crucial component in addiction recovery. By recognizing our powerlessness over addiction, we open ourselves up to a higher power that can guide us towards emotional and spiritual healing. We must surrender our ego and embrace humility to begin this journey.

Conclusion

Well, there you have it. The first step in addiction recovery is admitting we're powerless and acknowledging the unmanageability of our lives.

It's not easy, but it's necessary if we want to break free from addiction. Think of it like climbing a mountain. The first step is always the hardest, but once we get past it, the path becomes clearer.

We can't do it alone. We need support from others who have walked this path before us and are willing to guide us.

So let's take that first step together, admit our powerlessness, and embrace the journey towards recovery with open hearts and minds.

Remember: there's always hope for a better tomorrow, no matter how difficult it may seem right now.

STEP TWO

We Came To Believe That A Power Greater Than Ourselves Could Restore Us to Sanity

At the heart of addiction is a profound sense of powerlessness. We find ourselves caught in the grip of a disease that seems to have a will of its own, driving us towards self-destruction despite our best efforts to resist.

This is why Step Two of the 12-Step program is so crucial: it invites us to believe in something greater than ourselves that can restore us to sanity. For many of us, this concept can be challenging at first.

We may struggle with feelings of skepticism or reluctance, unsure if we are ready to surrender control and place our faith in something beyond our understanding. However, as we explore the nature of addiction as a disease and the limitations of human willpower in recovery, we begin to see the transformative power that spirituality can offer us.

In embracing Step Two, we open ourselves up to hope and healing – and discover that there is indeed a way out from under the weighty burden of addiction.

The Nature of Addiction as a Disease

You may have heard that addiction is a disease, but understanding the nature of this disease is crucial to overcoming it. Addiction isn't simply a lack of willpower or moral failing. It's a chronic brain disease that affects our ability to make rational decisions and control our impulses.

The brain changes that occur with addiction are complex and can be long-lasting. Repeated drug use alters the reward system in our brains, making us crave drugs even when we know they are harming us. This leads to compulsive drug seeking behavior and difficulty controlling drug use, despite negative consequences.

Recognizing addiction as a disease means acknowledging that we need help to overcome it. We can't simply will ourselves into recovery. Rather, we must seek out professional treatment and support from others who understand what we're going through.

In step two of the 12-step program, we come to believe that a power greater than ourselves can restore us to sanity. This means recognizing that we can't overcome addiction on our own and turning to a higher power for strength and guidance. By understanding addiction as a disease and seeking help from others, we can begin the journey towards recovery and restoring sanity in our lives.

The Limitations of Human Willpower in Recovery

Without help from something beyond your own strength, it can feel like trying to climb a mountain with no tools or equipment. This is especially true for those of us who've struggled with addiction.

We often find ourselves stuck in a cycle of relapse and recovery, unable to break free from the grip of our addiction on our own. The truth is, human willpower alone isn't enough to overcome addiction.

Our brains are wired in such a way that we become dependent on drugs or alcohol to function normally. Trying to quit cold turkey without any external support can be incredibly difficult, if not impossible.

That's where the second step comes in: "we came to believe that a power greater than ourselves could restore us to sanity."This doesn't necessarily mean belief in a higher power in the traditional sense; it could also refer to finding strength in community, therapy, or other forms of support.

The key is recognizing that we can't do this alone. As we begin to let go of our own limitations and trust in something beyond ourselves, we open ourselves up to the possibility of healing and recovery.

It takes courage and vulnerability to admit that we need help, but it's worth it when we start seeing progress towards a healthier life. So, if you're struggling with addiction, know that there's hope – and you don't have to do this alone.

The Concept of a Higher Power in 12-Step Programs

If you're looking for a way to find strength and support in addiction recovery, 12-step programs offer the concept of a higher power that can guide you towards healing. The idea is not to impose a specific religious belief on participants but rather to recognize that we are limited in our own ability to overcome addiction.

By acknowledging the existence of something more significant than ourselves, we open ourselves up to the possibility of change. Many people struggle with the concept of a higher power because it challenges their beliefs or lack thereof. However, it's essential to understand that this doesn't have to be a traditional deity or religious figure.

It could be anything that helps you connect with your inner self and give you hope and strength when things get tough. Some people find solace in nature or meditation, while others turn towards group therapy sessions where they can share their experiences and receive support.

The beauty of this approach is that it allows us to let go of our ego-driven desire for control and perfectionism. Instead, we accept that there are limitations to what we can accomplish alone, and we need help from something greater than ourselves. This shift in mindset requires humility and vulnerability, which can be difficult at first but ultimately leads us towards acceptance and peace.

The concept of a higher power is an integral part of 12-step programs because it provides us with hope, guidance, and strength as we navigate through addiction recovery. It's not about imposing any particular belief system on participants but rather recognizing our own limitations as human beings. By embracing something greater than ourselves, whether it's spiritual or not, we open up new possibilities for growth and healing.

Different Interpretations of a Higher Power

When exploring the concept of a higher power in 12-step programs, individuals may encounter various interpretations that go beyond traditional religious beliefs. For some, this higher power is simply the collective wisdom and experience of the group itself. Others see it as nature, the universe or even their own inner strength. Regardless of how one interprets it, the important thing is to recognize that there's something greater than ourselves that can help us overcome our addiction.

One interpretation of a higher power that resonates with many people in recovery is the idea of spirituality rather than religion. This means connecting with something greater than ourselves on a deep level, whether it be through meditation, prayer or other practices. It's about finding meaning and purpose in life beyond material possessions or physical pleasure.

Another popular interpretation of a higher power is the concept of karma – what goes around comes around. In this view, addiction is seen as a result of past actions and choices, and overcoming it requires making amends for those mistakes and trying to live in a more positive way. By doing good deeds and treating others with kindness and compassion, we can create positive energy that will ultimately come back to us.

Ultimately, what matters most when it comes to interpreting a higher power in 12-step programs is finding something that works for you personally. Whether you believe in God or not, there're plenty of ways to tap into something greater than yourself – from joining a support group to practicing mindfulness meditation. By opening yourself up to these possibilities and embracing your spiritual side (whatever form that takes), you can find hope and healing on your journey to recovery.

Surrendering to a Power Greater Than Oneself

You may feel hesitant to surrender to a power greater than yourself, but remember the story of the prodigal son who returned home and was welcomed with open arms. Surrendering to a power greater than ourselves isn't about giving up control or losing our individuality; it's about acknowledging that we can't do everything on our own. We need help, guidance, and support from something beyond ourselves. This is where faith comes in.

Faith can mean different things to different people, but at its core, it's about trusting in something bigger than oneself. It can be a higher power, nature, the universe, or even just the goodness of humanity. When we surrender to this faith and let go of our ego-driven desires for control and certainty, we open ourselves up to new possibilities and opportunities for growth.

Here are three ways that surrendering to a power greater than oneself can help restore sanity:

1. Letting go of perfectionism – Trying to control every aspect of our lives can lead to stress, anxiety, and burnout. Surrendering to a higher power means accepting that we're imperfect beings who make mistakes and have limitations.
2. Finding purpose – When we let go of our ego-driven desires for success and recognition, we create space for something greater than ourselves to guide us towards fulfilling our true purpose in life.
3. Connecting with others – Surrendering to a higher power means recognizing that we're all connected and interdependent beings. By letting go of selfish desires for personal gain or status, we open ourselves up to serving others and creating meaningful relationships based on compassion and empathy.

Surrendering to a power greater than oneself may seem intimidating at first but has enormous potential benefits for restoring sanity in one's life. Faith allows us to let go of control over everything in our lives while finding purpose through connection with other people around us!

The Role of Belief in Recovery

Belief is essential in the journey towards recovery, providing a sense of hope and purpose that can inspire individuals to overcome their struggles. It is through belief that we come to realize the possibility of becoming whole again, and the power that exists within us to make it happen.

When we believe in something greater than ourselves, we tap into a source of strength that can carry us through even the toughest times. In recovery, this belief often takes on a spiritual dimension. For many people, it involves surrendering to a Higher Power or God as they understand it. This act of surrendering allows them to let go of their own limitations and trust in something beyond themselves.

It may not be easy at first, but with time and practice, believing in this Power can bring about profound changes in our lives. One key aspect of this belief is recognizing that we cannot do everything on our own. We need help from others – whether it's other people who have gone through similar experiences or professional support like therapists or counselors.

By acknowledging our own limitations, we open ourselves up to receiving help from others and trusting in their expertise. Ultimately, the role of belief in recovery is about finding meaning and purpose beyond our struggles. It's about realizing that there is more to life than just getting by day-to-day – that we are capable of living fully and joyfully despite any challenges we may face.

With faith in something greater than ourselves guiding us forward, anything is possible.

Finding Hope in Step Two

Finding hope in Step Two involves recognizing the need for a power greater than ourselves. It's not just about acknowledging that we can't do it alone, but also understanding that there is something out there that can help us. This recognition is crucial to successful recovery, as research has shown that those who believe in a higher power are more likely to achieve long-term sobriety.

For some, finding this power may involve turning to religion or spirituality. For others, it may simply mean acknowledging the interconnectedness of all things and finding strength in the support of loved ones. Regardless of how we define our higher power, the important thing is that we recognize its presence and allow it to guide us on our journey towards healing.

It's important to note that Step Two does not require us to have a perfect understanding of our higher power right away. We don't need to know exactly what it is or how it works – we just need to be open to its existence and willing to let it help us.

As we continue on our path of recovery, we will inevitably develop a deeper understanding of what our higher power means to us. Ultimately, finding hope in Step Two means realizing that there is always a way out of addiction – no matter how hopeless things may seem at first.

By acknowledging the presence of a power greater than ourselves and allowing it to guide us towards healing, we can find renewed purpose and meaning in life beyond addiction.

Overcoming Reluctance to Embrace a Higher Power

After finding hope in Step Two, the next challenge is to overcome our reluctance to embrace a higher power. For many of us, this can be a difficult step because we may have had negative experiences with religion or spirituality in the past. We might also struggle with the idea of surrendering control and trusting in something outside of ourselves. However, it's important to remember that Step Two isn't about joining a particular religion or belief system - it's about recognizing that there's something greater than ourselves that can help us on our journey towards recovery.

1. Acknowledge your hesitation: It's okay if you're not ready to fully embrace a higher power right away. Take some time to explore your feelings and thoughts around spirituality and what it means for you personally. Talk to others who've gone through the same process and

ask for their advice.

2. Keep an open mind: You don't have to believe in a specific deity or even use the term 'God' if that doesn't resonate with you. The key is to remain open-minded and willing to consider all possibilities when it comes to what can restore us to sanity.
3. Look for evidence: Many people find that as they progress through their recovery journey, they begin to see signs of a higher power at work in their lives. Whether it's small coincidences or more significant events, pay attention to these moments and allow them to strengthen your faith.
4. Practice acceptance: Ultimately, embracing a higher power requires accepting that there are things outside of our control and trusting that everything will work out as it should. This can be challenging but practicing acceptance and letting go of our need for control can lead us towards greater peace and serenity.

Overcoming reluctance towards embracing a higher power isn't easy, but it's an essential part of finding lasting recovery from addiction or other challenges we may face in life. By acknowledging our hesitations, staying open-minded, looking for evidence, and practicing acceptance, we can move closer towards recognizing the power of something greater than ourselves. Trusting in this power can give us the strength and support we need to restore our sanity and live a fulfilling life in service to others.

Practical Steps for Putting Step Two into Action

To put Step Two into action, you can start by exploring your personal spirituality and keeping an open mind to the possibilities of what can guide you on your journey towards recovery. This may involve attending religious services or meditation classes, reading spiritual literature, or seeking out a trusted mentor who can offer guidance and support.

It's important to remember that there's no right or wrong way to approach spirituality - it's a deeply personal journey that will vary from person to person.

Another practical step for putting Step Two into action is to practice surrendering control over your addiction. This means acknowledging that you can't overcome your addiction through sheer willpower alone - you need the help of a power greater than yourself. Surrendering control may involve turning over your worries and fears to a higher power, practicing mindfulness and staying present in the moment, or developing gratitude for the blessings in your life.

A third step involves finding ways to stay connected with others who share similar struggles and beliefs. This may include joining a support group such as Alcoholics Anonymous (AA), Narcotics Anonymous (NA), or Celebrate Recovery. These groups provide a safe space where individuals can share their experiences, seek guidance from others who have been through similar struggles, and find strength in community.

It's important to remember that the process of coming to believe in a power greater than ourselves is not something that happens overnight - it's a gradual journey of self-discovery and growth. As we continue along this path, we may encounter setbacks and challenges along the way. However, by remaining committed to our recovery and remaining open-minded about our spiritual journeys, we can begin to trust in something greater than ourselves - whether it be God, nature, or simply the universe itself - to guide us towards lasting healing and peace of mind.

The Transformative Power of Spirituality in Recovery

You can experience a powerful transformation in your recovery when you embrace spirituality as a personal journey towards healing and growth. Spirituality isn't about religion, but about connecting with our inner selves and finding meaning in life beyond the physical realm.

In recovery, we often feel lost, hopeless, and disconnected from ourselves and others. However, when we begin to explore spirituality, we open ourselves up to new possibilities for healing and growth.

Here are some ways that spirituality can transform your recovery journey:

- It helps you find purpose: When we connect with our spiritual side, we begin to understand our true purpose in life. We realize that there's more to life than just material possessions or external achievements. This sense of purpose can provide us with the motivation to keep moving forward in our recovery journey.
- It fosters self-awareness: Spirituality encourages us to look within ourselves and confront our fears and shortcomings. By doing so, we become more self-aware and can identify patterns of behavior that may be hindering our progress in recovery.
- It promotes gratitude: Gratitude is an essential aspect of spirituality. When we focus on what we have instead of what we lack, we cultivate a positive mindset that helps us stay sober. Gratitude also allows us to appreciate the people around us who support us on our journey.
- It provides a sense of community: Many people find solace in joining spiritual communities such as churches or meditation groups during their recovery journey. These communities offer support and encouragement while fostering a sense of belonging.

Embracing spirituality can be an incredibly transformative experience for those seeking recovery from addiction or other mental health issues. By exploring your spiritual side through practices such as meditation or prayer, you can find meaning and purpose in life beyond your addiction. Moreover, by cultivating self-awareness and gratitude while fostering connections within a supportive community setting, you'll undoubtedly discover new possibilities for growth along the way!

Frequently Asked Questions

What are the specific steps involved in putting Step Two into action?

We start by admitting we're powerless over our addiction. Then, we come to believe that a Higher Power can restore us to sanity. We surrender to this power and ask for help as we continue on the path of recovery.

How does surrendering to a higher power help in addiction recovery?

Do we truly have the power to overcome addiction alone? Surrendering to a higher power allows us to let go of our ego and find humility, acceptance, and guidance in recovery.

Can someone in recovery choose not to believe in a higher power?

Yes, someone in recovery can choose not to believe in a higher power. However, our program emphasizes the importance of finding something greater than oneself to restore sanity and overcome addiction. It's up to each individual to interpret what that means for them.

What are some common misconceptions about the concept of a higher power in 12-step programs?

Common misconceptions about the higher power in 12-step programs include that it must be God or religious, and that it takes away personal responsibility. However, we believe that the higher power is a personal choice and can be anything greater than ourselves that helps us stay sober.

How can spirituality play a role in addiction recovery, and what does it entail?

Spirituality can play a vital role in addiction recovery, with studies showing that 73% of those who incorporate spirituality into their treatment experience positive outcomes. It involves connecting to a higher power and finding inner peace through practices like meditation, prayer, and mindfulness.

Conclusion

So there we have it, Step Two. It may seem like a daunting task to surrender to a power greater than ourselves, but it's essential in finding hope and restoring our sanity.

Just like a seed needs the nourishment of the sun and soil to grow into a beautiful flower, we need the guidance and support of something greater than us to overcome addiction.

Think of it like jumping out of an airplane with a parachute. We may feel scared and uncertain at first, but once we trust in the parachute to guide us safely down, we can experience the exhilarating freedom of soaring through the sky.

Embracing a higher power is like that parachuting experience - it takes courage and trust, but ultimately leads us to newfound freedom and happiness in recovery.

STEP THREE

We Made a Decision to Turn Our Will and Our Lives Over To the Care of God As We Understood Him

Imagine standing on the edge of a cliff, staring out at the vast expanse before you. You feel small and insignificant in comparison to the beauty and complexity of the world around you. This is how I felt when I first approached Step Three in my recovery journey. It was a moment of surrender, of acknowledging that there were forces beyond my control that could guide me towards healing and growth.

Step Three in the Twelve Step Program asks us to make a decision to turn our will and our lives over to the care of God as we understand Him. For some, this may seem like an impossible task - how can we trust something so intangible? But for others, it is a moment of relief, an opportunity to let go of the burden of control and allow something greater than ourselves to take charge.

In this article, we will explore the purpose behind Step Three, why surrendering control is so important in recovery, and different interpretations of what 'God' can mean in this context.

Understanding the Purpose of Step Three in the Twelve Step Program

Now, let's understand the purpose of Step Three in the Twelve Step Program and why we've made a decision to turn our will and our lives over to the care of God as we understand Him.

The purpose of Step Three is to surrender our self-will, ego, and selfishness to a higher power. We recognize that our own willpower wasn't enough to overcome addiction or other problems that brought us into recovery. By turning our will over to God, we're admitting that we need help from something greater than ourselves.

This step is crucial because it allows us to begin living a life free from the bondage of self. We learn that by letting go of control and trusting in a higher power, we can find peace and serenity. This doesn't mean that we become passive or stop taking responsibility for our actions; rather, it means that we accept what is out of our control and focus on what we can change.

Making this decision requires faith, but it doesn't necessarily require a specific religious belief system. The phrase 'as we understood Him' acknowledges that each person's concept of God may be different based on their individual experiences and beliefs. It's important for us to find a personal understanding of God or spirituality that resonates with us so that this step has meaning.

Step Three is about surrendering our self-will to something greater than ourselves so that we can live a more peaceful and fulfilling life. By accepting help from an external source beyond ourselves, whether it be through religion or spirituality or simply recognizing the interconnectedness of all things, we can break free from the cycle of addiction or other negative patterns in our lives.

Trusting in this process takes courage but opens up possibilities for growth and transformation beyond what we ever thought possible on our own.

The Importance of Surrendering Control in Recovery

Surrendering control is a crucial component of recovery, as it allows individuals to release their grip on the things that may be holding them back and trust in something greater than themselves.

This step asks us to acknowledge that we cannot do everything alone, and we need help from a power greater than ourselves. It's important to note that this power can be interpreted in many ways; for some, it may be God or a higher being, while for others, it could be nature or the universe.

To surrender control means admitting that our methods haven't been working and acknowledging the need for change. It's about accepting that we don't have all the answers and realizing there are limitations to what we can do on our own.

Once we let go of our ego-driven desire for complete control, we open ourselves up to new opportunities and possibilities.

When we make the decision to turn our will over to a higher power, it doesn't mean giving up responsibility or accountability. Rather, it means trusting in something greater than ourselves while also taking action towards positive change.

We must actively participate in our own recovery by doing things like attending meetings or therapy sessions and practicing self-care.

Overall, surrendering control is essential because it allows us to let go of past mistakes and focus on moving forward with hope and positivity. By admitting that there are aspects of life beyond our control, we free ourselves from unnecessary stressors and pave the way for personal growth.

Trusting in a higher power helps us find peace amidst chaos and empowers us to serve others with compassion.

The Role of a Higher Power in the Recovery Process

Trusting in a higher power can provide individuals with the strength and guidance needed to overcome challenges and maintain sobriety. For many people, turning their will and lives over to a power greater than themselves is an essential step in the recovery process.

The idea of surrendering control can be scary, but it's important to remember that we don't have to take on everything alone. One of the most significant benefits of having trust in a higher power is that it allows us to let go of our fears and worries.

When we acknowledge that there are things beyond our control, we can stop trying to force outcomes and instead focus on doing what we can in the present moment. This mindset enables us to approach life with more peace and acceptance, which can be incredibly helpful for staying grounded during tough times.

Another way that relying on a higher power can help with recovery is by providing structure and purpose. Many people find meaning in connecting with something larger than themselves, whether it's through prayer, meditation, or simply spending time outdoors enjoying nature.

Having a sense of purpose outside ourselves can give us motivation and direction as we work towards building a better life for ourselves. Ultimately, turning our wills over to a higher power is about recognizing our limitations as human beings and trusting that there is something greater at work in the world around us.

Whether you believe in God or not, this practice encourages humility, gratitude, and compassion - all qualities that are essential for living a fulfilling life. By embracing this step in the recovery process, individuals open themselves up to new possibilities for growth and transformation.

Different Interpretations of God in Step Three

You may have different ideas of who or what your higher power is, whether it's a traditional deity or simply a force of nature that gives you guidance and strength like the wind at your back. In step three, we make a conscious decision to turn our will and our lives over to this higher power as we understand it. This may be difficult for some, especially if they've had negative experiences with religion or spirituality.

However, the beauty of the program is that each person can interpret their higher power in their own way. Here are some common interpretations of a higher power in step three:

- A traditional deity: For many people, God as described in religious texts is the ultimate higher power. They find comfort in praying to this God and seeking guidance from holy books.
- Nature: Others see their higher power as something found in nature. The beauty of the world around them reminds them that there is something greater than themselves at work.
- Inner strength: Some people believe that their higher power comes from within themselves. They tap into an inner reserve of strength and resilience when faced with challenges.

Regardless of how someone interprets their higher power, step three requires surrendering control over one's life to this force. It takes humility and trust to let go and allow oneself to be guided by something outside of oneself.

In serving others, we can also find inspiration for our understanding of a higher power. When we witness acts of kindness or selflessness, it can remind us that there is goodness in the world beyond ourselves. By turning our will over to this goodness, we become part of something greater than ourselves and find purpose in helping others along their journey towards recovery.

Overcoming Resistance to Step Three

When resistance to the idea of a higher power arises, it can feel like standing at the edge of a cliff, unsure of what lies beyond. Surrendering control and turning our will over to something outside of ourselves can be frightening. It requires us to let go of our ego and admit that we can't do everything on our own.

However, once we take this step, we find that it brings immense relief. We no longer have to bear the weight of the world on our shoulders. We can trust that there's a force greater than ourselves guiding us in the right direction. This frees up space for us to focus on serving others and making positive changes in our lives.

The key to overcoming resistance is finding a version of God or a higher power that resonates with us personally. It doesn't matter if it's traditional religion or something more abstract like nature or the universe. What matters is having faith in something bigger than ourselves and being willing to let go of control.

Taking Step Three may seem daunting at first, but it ultimately leads to freedom and peace of mind. By surrendering control and trusting in a higher power, we open ourselves up to new possibilities and opportunities for growth. So let's embrace Step Three with an open heart and mind, knowing that it'll bring us closer to living fulfilling lives as we serve others around us.

Letting Go of Ego and Embracing Humility

Letting go of our ego and embracing humility is a challenging but essential part of recovery. Studies show that individuals with higher levels of humility have greater psychological well-being and life satisfaction. It requires us to recognize that we do not have all the answers and we cannot control every aspect of our lives. By acknowledging this, we open ourselves up to the possibility of receiving help from a power greater than ourselves.

Here are four ways in which letting go of ego and embracing humility can benefit us on our recovery journey:

1. Increased self-awareness: When we let go of our ego, we become more aware of our flaws and shortcomings. This allows us to take an honest inventory of ourselves and work towards improving those areas.
2. Improved relationships: Humility allows us to be more receptive to others' perspectives, leading to better communication and stronger relationships. We learn how to listen without judgment and respond with empathy.
3. Greater sense of purpose: By surrendering our will to a higher power, we find meaning in serving others rather than just focusing on ourselves. This gives us a sense of purpose beyond material possessions or personal achievements.
4. Inner peace: Letting go of the need for control can bring about a sense of inner peace that transcends any external circumstances. We learn how to trust in something greater than ourselves and find comfort in knowing that everything happens for a reason.

Step three requires us to let go of our ego and embrace humility so that we can turn our will over to God as we understand him. By doing so, we gain increased self-awareness, improved relationships, greater sense of purpose, and inner peace - all crucial elements on the road towards recovery. It's important that we continue practicing these principles even after completing step three, as they play an integral role in maintaining long-term sobriety while serving others along the way.

Making a Conscious Decision to Trust in a Higher Power

Making a conscious choice to trust in something greater than ourselves can be a difficult but rewarding step towards recovery. It requires us to let go of the need for control and acknowledge that we can't do everything on our own.

This can be especially challenging for those of us who've always relied on our own abilities to navigate through life. However, when we make the decision to turn our will and our lives over to the care of God as we understand him, we open ourselves up to an entirely new way of living.

For many of us, this means accepting that there's a power greater than ourselves at work in the universe. We recognize that while we may not know exactly what this power looks like or how it operates, we trust that it has our best interests at heart. This faith allows us to surrender control and find peace in knowing that things will unfold as they're meant to.

Turning our lives over to a higher power also means letting go of old patterns and behaviors that no longer serve us. We become willing to take actions that align with this new way of living, even if they're uncomfortable or unfamiliar at first.

This process often involves working with others who share similar beliefs and values, as well as seeking guidance from spiritual leaders or mentors.

In making the decision to trust in something greater than ourselves, we open ourselves up to endless possibilities for growth and transformation. By humbly acknowledging our limitations and embracing a willingness to change, we allow space for miracles and blessings beyond anything we could have imagined on our own.

And ultimately, by serving others through this process, we find fulfillment in ways that exceed anything self-seeking behavior could ever provide.

The Benefits of Turning over Will and Life to a Higher Power

Surrendering control to a higher power can bring incredible benefits and opportunities for growth. When we make the decision to turn our will and our lives over to God, we open ourselves up to new possibilities we may have never considered before.

Here are some of the ways turning over control can benefit us:

- We become more open-minded. When we let go of the need to control everything around us, we become more receptive to ideas and perspectives that differ from our own. We start seeing the world through a wider lens, allowing us to learn and grow in ways that were previously impossible.
- We feel less anxious. When we try to control every aspect of our lives, it can lead to feelings of overwhelm and anxiety. But when we surrender control and trust in a higher power, those feelings begin to dissipate. We realize that there is something bigger than ourselves guiding us along our journey.
- We become more compassionate. Once we let go of our need for control, we begin to see others in a different light as well. Instead of judging or criticizing them for their choices or behaviors, we develop empathy and understanding for their struggles.

By turning over our will and life to a higher power, we trust in something greater than ourselves. This act alone can be incredibly empowering because it frees us from the burden of trying to navigate life on our own. It allows us to tap into an inner strength that comes from knowing that no matter what happens, things will work out as they should.

When you make this decision for yourself, remember that it doesn't mean you're giving up your personal power or autonomy. Rather, it's about acknowledging your limitations as a human being and recognizing the value in seeking guidance beyond yourself. So take comfort in knowing that by turning your will and life over to God (or whatever higher power you choose), you are opening yourself up to a world of possibilities and opportunities for growth.

Implementing Step Three in Daily Life

Implementing Step Three in daily life can be challenging, but studies show that those who trust in a higher power have lower levels of stress and anxiety. It's important to remember that turning our will and lives over to a higher power doesn't mean we're giving up control of our lives. Instead, it means we're acknowledging that there are things beyond our control and trusting that a higher power will guide us through them.

One way to implement Step Three is by starting the day with prayer or meditation. This helps us focus on what's truly important and reminds us that we're not alone in our struggles.

We can also take time throughout the day to pause and reflect on our actions, asking ourselves if they align with our values and the guidance of our higher power.

Another aspect of implementing Step Three is being open to change. When we turn our will over to a higher power, we're accepting that there may be different paths for us than what we originally planned. It can be difficult to let go of certain goals or expectations, but trusting in a higher power can lead us towards new opportunities that ultimately serve a greater purpose.

Implementing Step Three involves cultivating an attitude of gratitude. By recognizing the blessings in our lives, both big and small, we become more aware of how much support and love surrounds us. This helps us approach challenges with more resilience and optimism.

Overall, implementing Step Three requires patience, humility, and faith. By surrendering control over what is beyond our capacity to manage on our own while actively working towards positive outcomes within it under divine guidance makes this step fulfilling for anyone who embraces it wholeheartedly.

Moving Forward in Recovery with Step Three as a Foundation

As you continue on your recovery journey, Step Three serves as a solid foundation to build upon. This step is about making a conscious decision to let go of our own will and trust in a higher power. It can be difficult to surrender control, especially for those who've always tried to manage everything themselves. However, by turning our lives over to the care of God as we understand him, we open ourselves up to new possibilities and opportunities for growth.

Moving forward with Step Three as our foundation means taking action towards our goals and trusting that things will work out as they're meant to. This doesn't mean sitting back and waiting for things to happen; rather, it's about actively participating in life while remaining open and receptive to the guidance of a higher power.

By doing so, we cultivate a sense of faith that helps us navigate life's challenges with more grace and ease. One way to deepen our connection with a higher power is through prayer or meditation. These practices help us quiet our minds and tune into something greater than ourselves. They also allow us to tap into an inner wisdom that can guide us towards making choices that align with our values and purpose in life.

It's important to remember that recovery is not just about helping ourselves but also about serving others. When we make the decision to turn our lives over to the care of God as we understand him, it opens up opportunities for us to be of service in ways that align with our values and strengths.

By giving back and helping others on their own journeys towards recovery, we create meaning and purpose in our own lives while also contributing positively to the world around us.

Frequently Asked Questions

What are some common misconceptions about Step Three and surrendering to a higher power?

Many believe Step Three requires a rigid adherence to religion or deity worship. However, we've found the surrender to a higher power is personal and individualized. It's about releasing control and finding humility in the face of addiction.

How can someone who doesn't believe in God or a higher power approach Step Three?

For those who don't believe in a higher power, Step Three can still be approached by surrendering to something greater than ourselves. We can turn our will over to the care of our inner voice or the collective good.

Can someone who has already turned their life over to a higher

power still struggle with Step Three?

Even if we've already surrendered to a higher power, Step Three can still be challenging. It requires ongoing commitment to trust and rely on something beyond ourselves, which can be difficult at times.

How can someone maintain their own agency and decision-making while also turning their will and life over to a higher power?

As we strive to turn our lives over to a higher power, it's important to remember that we still have agency and decision-making abilities. By surrendering our will, we gain the strength and guidance needed to serve others and live a purposeful life.

How does Step Three relate to other steps in the Twelve Step program, such as Step One (admitting powerlessness) and Step Two (believing in a higher power)?

Step Three builds upon the acknowledgement of powerlessness in Step One and belief in a higher power in Step Two. By making a decision to turn our will and lives over, we open ourselves up to guidance and support from that higher power.

Conclusion

In conclusion, Step Three of the Twelve Step Program is a crucial component in achieving long-term recovery. By surrendering our will and lives over to a higher power, we acknowledge that we can't do it alone and need help from something greater than ourselves.

This act of humility can be difficult but ultimately leads to freedom from addiction. Symbolically speaking, turning our will and life over to a higher power is like handing over the reins of a wild horse to someone who knows how to tame it.

We let go of control and trust in the guidance of a power greater than ourselves. In doing so, we find peace and serenity in our daily lives as we navigate through challenges with newfound strength and resilience.

Embracing Step Three allows us to move forward in recovery with an open mind, heart, and spirit – ready for whatever lies ahead on this journey towards healing.

STEP FOUR

We Made a Searching and Fearless Moral Inventory of Ourselves

As we move through the 12-step program of addiction recovery, Step Four is a crucial turning point. In this step, we are asked to make a searching and fearless moral inventory of ourselves.

This means taking an honest look at our past behaviors, character defects, resentments, fears, and mistakes in order to gain a clearer understanding of who we are and how these factors may have contributed to our addiction.

At first glance, this task may seem daunting or even overwhelming. However, it is important to remember that Step Four is not about self-punishment or dwelling on past mistakes.

Rather, it is a vital step towards personal growth and healing. By confronting our shortcomings head-on and acknowledging their impact on our lives and relationships, we can begin to develop a stronger foundation for recovery and build healthier habits moving forward.

The Purpose of Step Four in Addiction Recovery

The purpose of step four in addiction recovery is to delve into a searching and fearless moral inventory of ourselves. This step is crucial as it requires us to take a hard look at our past behaviors, attitudes, and beliefs that have contributed to our addiction.

It's an opportunity for us to identify our character defects and acknowledge the harm we've caused others. When we make a searching and fearless moral inventory of ourselves, we're essentially taking responsibility for our actions.

We can't change what we don't acknowledge, so this step gives us the chance to be honest with ourselves about who we are and how we've impacted those around us. It's not an easy task, but it's necessary if we want to move forward in recovery.

By examining our past behaviors and attitudes, we can begin to make amends with those whom we've harmed. We can also start rebuilding trust with ourselves and others by recognizing where we fell short in the past.

When done properly, this step helps us gain insight into why we turned to substances in the first place so that we can work towards finding healthier coping mechanisms. Ultimately, making a searching and fearless moral inventory of ourselves is an act of self-love.

It takes courage and vulnerability to face our shortcomings head-on, but doing so allows us to become better versions of ourselves. Through this process, we can learn from our mistakes and begin living a life free from addiction while serving as an example for others on their own journey towards recovery.

Understanding the Importance of Self-Reflection

To truly understand the importance of self-reflection, you must take a deep and honest look at your own thoughts, actions, and beliefs. It's not always easy to confront our flaws or explore the darker corners of our minds, but it's essential for growth and healing.

Here are some reasons why self-reflection is so important:

- Self-awareness: By examining our own behavior and thought patterns, we gain a deeper understanding of who we are as individuals. We can identify our strengths and weaknesses, recognize harmful habits and triggers, and develop strategies for improving ourselves.
- Empathy: When we reflect on our own experiences and challenges, we become more compassionate towards others who may be going through similar struggles. We also learn to listen more attentively and communicate more effectively with those around us.
- Accountability: Taking responsibility for our actions is a crucial part of personal growth. Through self-reflection, we can acknowledge any harm we may have caused others or ourselves in the past, make amends where necessary, and commit to making positive changes moving forward.
- Gratitude: Reflecting on all that we have to be grateful for can help us maintain a positive outlook even during challenging times. It's easy to get bogged down by negativity or stressors in life; taking time to focus on what brings us joy can help shift our perspective.

By making an inventory of ourselves in Step Four of addiction recovery, we're essentially conducting an extensive self-reflection process. This allows us to identify any negative patterns or behaviors that contributed to addictive behaviors in the past - such as avoidance or denial - so that we can address them head-on.

While this step may feel daunting at first glance, it's ultimately empowering because it puts us back in control of our lives. Through honest self-examination, accountability becomes possible; with accountability comes the opportunity for lasting change.

Reflection isn't just navel-gazing or wallowing in self-pity - it's an essential component of personal growth and healing. By examining our own thoughts, actions, and beliefs with honesty and compassion, we can gain a deeper understanding of ourselves while also becoming more empathetic towards others.

In addiction recovery, Step Four allows us to take this process even further by identifying harmful patterns that may have contributed to addictive behaviors in the past. Ultimately, self-reflection is about taking responsibility for ourselves and committing to living our best lives possible - not just for our own sake but for those around us as well.

Identifying Character Defects and Negative Behaviors

You must face your own character defects and negative behaviors head-on if you want to truly heal from addiction. This step requires honesty, openness, and willingness to identify the things that have been holding us back.

It's important to remember that we're not perfect and we all have flaws. Once we accept this fact, we can begin the process of identifying our shortcomings. Identifying our character defects and negative behaviors is a challenging task.

It requires us to take an honest look at ourselves and acknowledge where we've gone wrong in the past. We may need to confront some uncomfortable truths about ourselves, but it's necessary for growth. By doing so, we can gain insight into why we behave in certain ways and make changes for the better.

The inventory process involves taking a hard look at our resentments, fears, and harms done to others. We must be willing to admit when we're wrong and take responsibility for our actions. This allows us to move forward without being held back by guilt or shame from past mistakes.

Through this self-reflection process, we can develop a deeper sense of empathy towards others as well as ourselves. Making a searching and fearless moral inventory of ourselves is a crucial step in addiction recovery.

It allows us to identify areas where we need improvement while also gaining insight into what makes us tick as individuals. By confronting our character defects head-on, with honesty and self-compassion, we can pave the way towards true healing and personal growth.

Examining Resentments and Their Impact

Examining our resentments and how they've impacted us can be uncomfortable, but it's an important step in addiction recovery that can lead to healing and personal growth. Resentment is often a result of unmet expectations or perceived injustices. It's easy to get caught up in the negative feelings associated with resentment, but taking the time to examine these emotions can help us identify patterns of behavior that have been holding us back.

When we make a searching and fearless moral inventory of ourselves, one of the key areas we need to explore is our resentments. This involves identifying who or what we are resentful towards, why we feel this way, and how it has affected our thoughts and actions. By doing this, we can gain insight into our own character defects and negative behaviors.

Here are some ways that examining our resentments can help us in addiction recovery:

- It allows us to take responsibility for our own emotions: When we recognize that our resentments are often a result of unmet expectations or perceived injustices, we can begin to take ownership over how we react to these situations.
- It helps us develop empathy: By understanding the root causes behind other people's actions (even if they were hurtful), we can begin to see things from their perspective and develop more compassion towards others.
- It fosters forgiveness: Examining our own role in conflicts and acknowledging any harm that may have been caused allows us to let go of anger and move towards forgiveness.
- It promotes self-awareness: By being honest with ourselves about our own character defects and negative behaviors, we can begin to work on changing them for the better.

Overall, examining our resentments is an important part of making a searching and fearless moral inventory as it enables us to gain insight into ourselves and promotes personal growth. By doing so, we become more equipped with tools necessary for serving others on their journey towards healing from addiction.

Addressing Fears and Their Role in Addiction

Addressing our fears is crucial in addiction recovery as they often play a significant role in perpetuating addictive behaviors that prevent us from reaching our full potential and living a fulfilling life. Fear can manifest itself in many ways, such as fear of failure, fear of rejection, or fear of the unknown. These fears can drive individuals to turn to drugs or alcohol as a way to cope with their emotions.

The fourth step in the 12-step program encourages individuals to make a searching and fearless moral inventory of themselves. This means taking an honest look at ourselves and identifying our character defects, including the fears that hold us back from living our best lives. By acknowledging these fears, we become better equipped to deal with them and find healthy ways to manage them.

It's important to remember that addressing our fears is not a one-time event but rather an ongoing process throughout recovery. We must continually examine ourselves and be willing to face uncomfortable truths about ourselves if we want to continue growing and healing from addiction.

Facing our fears is essential for anyone seeking long-term recovery from addiction. By actively working on this step in the 12-step program, we can develop stronger coping mechanisms for dealing with stressors that would have previously led us down the path of substance abuse. Ultimately, by confronting these fears head-on, we can achieve a greater sense of self-awareness and move towards living happier, healthier lives free from addiction.

Confronting Harmful Habits and Addictive Triggers

When it comes to confronting harmful habits and addictive triggers, it's like navigating a minefield - one wrong step can set you off course and lead to relapse. That's why making a searching and fearless moral inventory of ourselves is such an important step in addiction recovery.

It allows us to identify the root causes of our addictive behavior, including harmful habits and triggers that we need to confront head-on. Making this inventory requires us to take a hard look at ourselves, including our character defects, past mistakes, and areas where we've caused harm to others.

This type of self-reflection can be difficult, but it's necessary for growth and healing. By acknowledging the ways in which we've fallen short in the past, we're able to make amends with those we've hurt and work towards becoming better versions of ourselves.

In addition to addressing our own shortcomings, making a thorough inventory also involves examining external factors that may contribute to our addiction. This includes identifying people, places or things that trigger cravings or negative emotions.

By understanding these triggers and learning how to manage them effectively through healthy coping mechanisms (such as mindfulness practices), we can reduce the risk of relapse. Overall, making a searching and fearless moral inventory of ourselves is an integral part of addiction recovery.

It allows us to confront harmful habits head-on while also developing greater insight into our own selves. With this knowledge in hand, we're able to move forward on the path towards lasting healing and transformation.

Taking Responsibility for Past Mistakes

It's time to own up to our past mistakes and take responsibility for the harm we've caused. This is a crucial step in making a searching and fearless moral inventory of ourselves. It requires us to look back on our actions with honesty, humility, and a willingness to learn from our mistakes.

Taking responsibility for past mistakes means acknowledging the harm we've caused others and making amends where possible. It also means being accountable for the consequences of our actions, both good and bad.

By doing so, we can begin to repair damaged relationships, restore trust, and move forward with integrity.

This process can be difficult and uncomfortable, but it's necessary for personal growth and spiritual development. It requires us to confront our own shortcomings, face our fears, and embrace vulnerability.

But by doing so, we gain a deeper understanding of ourselves and others, develop empathy and compassion, and become better equipped to serve those around us.

In taking responsibility for past mistakes, we also demonstrate a commitment to living a life of purpose and meaning. We recognize that our actions have an impact on those around us, both positive or negative.

And by owning up to our mistakes with sincerity and humility, we show that we are committed to serving others with compassion, kindness, and respect.

Developing a Clearer Sense of Self

To get a clearer sense of who we are, it's important to take the time to reflect on our values and beliefs. Understanding what drives us and how we make decisions is crucial in developing a stronger sense of self. This process can be challenging at times, but it ultimately leads to personal growth and self-awareness.

One way we can reflect on our values and beliefs is by examining our past actions and decisions. By taking responsibility for our mistakes, we can learn from them and avoid repeating them in the future. This requires honesty with ourselves, which is essential for the next step in the recovery process: making a searching and fearless moral inventory of ourselves.

When we conduct this inventory, we are essentially taking an honest look at who we are as individuals. We examine our character defects as well as our positive attributes. This step requires courage because it means confronting uncomfortable truths about ourselves that may have been buried deep within us for years.

However, by conducting this inventory with honesty and openness, we gain a better understanding of ourselves - both the good and the bad. This understanding allows us to continue growing as individuals, making better choices aligned with our values, beliefs, and ultimately serving others around us in a more meaningful way than just living life without purpose or direction.

Applying Step Four to Daily Life

By confronting our flaws and recognizing our strengths, we can integrate the lessons learned from Step Four into our daily lives and become more self-aware individuals.

This step requires us to take a deep dive into ourselves and examine every aspect of our lives, including the good, bad, and ugly. It's not an easy process, but it's necessary for personal growth.

The key to applying Step Four to daily life is to be honest with ourselves about who we are and what motivates us. We must acknowledge the areas in which we fall short and take responsibility for our actions. This includes taking inventory of past mistakes or hurtful behavior towards others. By doing so, we become more accountable for our actions and can work towards making amends with those we have wronged.

While this may seem daunting at first, it's important to remember that self-reflection can lead to positive change in all aspects of our lives. By identifying patterns in our behavior, we can begin to understand why certain situations trigger negative reactions or emotions within us. Through this understanding, we can then develop healthier coping mechanisms that allow us to navigate challenging situations without falling back into old habits.

By completing Step Four with honesty and introspection, we open ourselves up to greater self-awareness and personal growth in all areas of our lives. While it may be uncomfortable at times, the end result is worth the effort as it allows us to live more fulfilling lives while serving others from a place of emotional maturity and compassion.

Moving Forward with a Stronger Foundation for Recovery

Now that we've taken the time to examine our flaws and strengths, we can move forward with a stronger foundation for recovery.

The fourth step isn't just about identifying our character defects; it's also about taking responsibility for them. We can't change what we refuse to acknowledge. By making a searching and fearless moral inventory of ourselves, we open ourselves up to growth and progress.

It's important to remember that this step is not a one-time event; it's an ongoing process. As we continue on our recovery journey, new character defects may surface, and it's up to us to recognize them and take action. This can be challenging at times, but the rewards are worth it.

By continually working on ourselves, we become better people overall.

Moving forward with a stronger foundation for recovery means being honest with ourselves and others. It means taking accountability for our actions and making amends when necessary. It also means being willing to forgive ourselves and others when mistakes are made. By doing these things, we create an atmosphere of trust and respect within our recovery community.

The fourth step is a crucial part of the recovery process as it allows us to understand who we truly are as individuals. Moving forward with a stronger foundation for recovery requires us to be open-minded, honest, accountable, forgiving, and willing to grow continuously.

As long as we stay committed to this process of self-discovery and improvement, there's no limit to what we can achieve in life!

Frequently Asked Questions

What is the history or origin of Step Four in addiction recovery programs?

Step Four in addiction recovery programs has its roots in the Oxford Group, a religious movement that emphasized personal inventory. It helps us examine our character defects and take responsibility for our actions, leading to personal growth and a better life.

How long should a person spend on their moral inventory during Step Four?

During Step Four, we should take the time needed to conduct a thorough moral inventory of ourselves. Rushing through this process could lead to incomplete or inaccurate results, ultimately hindering our recovery progress.

What is the success rate of individuals who complete Step Four in addiction recovery programs?

The success rate of individuals who complete step four in addiction recovery programs varies. However, as we focus on serving others and confront our past behavior, the emotional response can be powerful, leading to positive change.

Are there any negative side effects or risks associated with completing Step Four?

There are no negative side effects or risks associated with completing Step Four in addiction recovery programs. Instead, it offers a chance for growth and self-discovery, leading to a better understanding of ourselves and our behaviors.

How can someone determine if they have adequately completed their moral inventory during Step Four?

To determine if we've completed our moral inventory, we must ask ourselves if we've been honest and thorough in examining our faults and shortcomings. We can't sweep anything under the rug; it's time to face the music.

Conclusion

In conclusion, Step Four of addiction recovery is a pivotal moment in the journey towards lasting sobriety. By taking an honest and thorough inventory of ourselves, we can identify the negative behaviors and character defects that have contributed to our addictive tendencies.

Through this process, we gain greater self-awareness and develop a clearer sense of who we are as individuals. To use a metaphor, Step Four is like shining a light into the darkest corners of our soul.

It may be uncomfortable and challenging at times, but ultimately it allows us to see ourselves more clearly and make necessary changes for personal growth. By embracing this step with courage and openness, we lay the foundation for a brighter future filled with purpose and fulfillment.

STEP FIVE

We Admitted To God, To Ourselves, And To another Human Being the Exact Nature of Our Wrongs

Well, well, well. Here we are at Step Five of the recovery process. Are you ready to confront your demons and face the music? Because that's what this step is all about - admitting to God, ourselves, and another human being the exact nature of our wrongs.

It may sound daunting (and let's be honest, it is), but it's also one of the most crucial steps in our journey towards sobriety and growth. It's a chance for us to take a long hard look in the mirror and acknowledge our shortcomings, flaws, and mistakes without judgment or shame.

So grab a chair and get comfortable - we're about to dive deep into the purpose of Step Five and how it can help us become better versions of ourselves.

The Purpose of Step Five in Recovery

Now, you're ready to dive deeper into your recovery by admitting to God, yourself, and another person the specific details of your wrongdoings in step five. This step is a crucial part of recovery as it helps us understand the exact nature of our wrongs and take responsibility for them. It's an opportunity to be honest with ourselves and others about our past actions.

The purpose of Step Five is not only to acknowledge our mistakes but also to seek forgiveness and make amends where possible. By sharing our wrongdoings with another person, we can gain a different perspective on our behavior and receive guidance on how to move forward. Admission leads us towards acceptance, which is essential for personal growth and change.

Admitting our faults may seem daunting at first, but it's important to remember that this step isn't about judgment or punishment. Rather, it's a chance for us to let go of the shame that has been holding us back from living a fulfilling life. By surrendering ourselves to a higher power and admitting our mistakes without reservation, we can find peace within ourselves.

Step Five allows us to come clean about the things we've done wrong in order to reconcile with those we've hurt and move forward in sobriety. It's an opportunity for self-reflection and humility that ultimately leads us towards healing.

Remember that admitting our wrongdoing isn't easy but is necessary for true freedom from addiction – we're all works in progress striving towards becoming better versions of ourselves every day.

Confronting and Acknowledging Our Shortcomings

As we confront and acknowledge our own shortcomings, it's important to remember the famous quote by Maya Angelou: 'Do the best you can until you know better. Then when you know better, do better.'

This step is about taking responsibility for our actions and being honest with ourselves and others. It's not an easy process, but it's necessary for growth and recovery.

Here are five things to keep in mind as we take this step:

- Be courageous: Admitting our wrongs takes courage. We have to face our fears of rejection, judgment, and shame. But by doing so, we give ourselves the opportunity for healing and forgiveness.
- Be specific: It's not enough to say 'I was selfish' or 'I lied.' We need to be specific about what we did wrong and how it affected others. This helps us see the impact of our actions and make amends where possible.
- Be accountable: We can't blame others for our mistakes or justify our behavior. We have to take ownership of what we've done and accept the consequences.
- Be compassionate: Remember that admitting our wrongs doesn't make us bad people; it makes us human. We all make mistakes, but it's how we learn from them that matters.
- Be willing: This step requires a willingness to change. We can't keep doing the same things and expect different results. By admitting our wrongs, we open ourselves up to new possibilities for growth and transformation.

Step Five is about confronting and acknowledging our shortcomings with courage, specificity, accountability, compassion, and willingness. It's a difficult but necessary part of the recovery process that allows us to grow as individuals while serving others in a positive way. As Maya Angelou reminds us: 'When you know better, do better.'

Understanding the Importance of Admitting Our Wrongs

Understanding the importance of acknowledging your mistakes takes courage and a willingness to change, allowing you to grow as an individual and positively impact those around you. It's easy to ignore our faults and make excuses for them, but doing so only hinders our personal growth.

Admitting our wrongs means taking responsibility for our actions, which can be uncomfortable at times. However, it's important to remember that we aren't perfect beings and that making mistakes is a natural part of life.

When we admit to God, ourselves, and another human being the exact nature of our wrongs, we're taking a big step towards healing. This confession allows us to release the burden of guilt and shame that come with holding onto past mistakes. When we acknowledge our wrongdoings, it becomes easier for us to forgive ourselves and move forward in a positive direction.

Admitting our wrongs also helps us build stronger relationships with those around us. By being honest about our shortcomings, we show others that we value their trust and respect enough to be vulnerable with them. In turn, this vulnerability creates deeper connections between individuals who are committed to supporting each other through their struggles.

Admitting our wrongs is an essential step towards personal growth and building meaningful relationships with others. It requires courage and humility but is ultimately worth it in the end. By embracing honesty about ourselves while serving others' subconscious desires for kindness, we will lead ourselves on the path towards becoming better versions of ourselves while impacting those around us positively.

Overcoming the Fear of Admitting Our Wrongs

Admitting our mistakes can be scary, but it's important to remember that growth and healing come from vulnerability. When we admit our wrongs to another human being, we are opening ourselves up to the possibility of judgment and rejection.

However, it's crucial to understand that this fear is often rooted in a desire for control. We want to control how others perceive us and avoid the discomfort of facing our flaws head-on.

Overcoming this fear requires a willingness to let go of control and trust in the process of growth. It means acknowledging that we are not perfect beings and that making mistakes is a natural part of life.

By admitting our wrongs, we invite others into our journey towards self-improvement. Moreover, admitting our wrongs can also help us develop stronger relationships with those around us. When we open up about our struggles, we allow others to see us as more than just the sum of our actions.

We become relatable human beings with whom others can connect on a deeper level. While admitting our wrongs may be scary, it is an essential step towards personal growth and building meaningful connections with others.

By letting go of control and embracing vulnerability, we allow ourselves the opportunity for true healing and transformation.

Choosing the Right Person to Confide In

Finding someone you can trust and confide in is crucial for emotional healing and growth. When we admit our wrongs to another person, it can be a difficult and vulnerable experience. However, choosing the right person to confide in can make all the difference in our recovery journey.

Here are some things to consider when selecting someone to share your struggles with:

- **Trustworthiness:** Look for someone who's proven themselves trustworthy in the past. This could be a close friend or family member, or even a therapist or counselor.
- **Empathy:** It's important to choose someone who'll listen without judgment and offer empathy and support. This could be someone who's been through similar experiences themselves or simply has a compassionate nature.
- **Confidentiality:** Make sure you choose someone who understands the importance of confidentiality. You want to feel safe sharing your deepest thoughts and fears without worrying about them being shared with others.
- **Availability:** Choose someone who's available when you need them most. Whether it's a designated time each week or simply having an open-door policy, feeling like you have access to support can make all the difference.
- **Non-judgmental attitude:** Finally, look for someone who maintains a non-judgmental attitude towards you as well as your situation.

When we find the right person to confide in, admitting our wrongs becomes less scary and more cathartic. The act of speaking our truth out loud allows us to release shame and guilt that may have been weighing us down for years.

Additionally, allowing ourselves to be vulnerable with another person creates deeper connections and fosters greater understanding between individuals.

Finding the right person to admit our wrongs to is crucial for emotional healing and growth. By considering traits such as trustworthiness, empathy, confidentiality, availability, and non-judgmental attitudes when selecting this individual, we increase our chances of experiencing meaningful change.

Admitting our wrongs can be a difficult journey, but with the right person by our side, we can find strength in vulnerability and move towards a more fulfilling life.

Preparing for the Admission Process

Before we dive into the process of admitting our wrongdoings, let's take a moment to acknowledge that it won't be easy. It takes real courage to confront our mistakes and share them with someone else. However, this step is crucial in the recovery process because it allows us to take responsibility for our actions and move forward towards healing.

Preparing for the admission process involves taking an honest inventory of our past behaviors and identifying where we've fallen short. This can be a difficult task as it requires us to face uncomfortable truths about ourselves. We may feel shame, guilt, or fear when looking at our past actions, but it's important to remember that admitting faults is not a sign of weakness but rather strength.

Once we've identified areas where we need to make amends, it's time to choose someone who we trust and respect enough to confide in. This person should be non-judgmental, willing to listen actively and understand without bias or criticism. It could be a close friend, family member, or even a counselor.

When approaching this conversation with another human being, it's important that we choose our words carefully. We must be honest about what happened while also taking ownership of how our behavior has impacted others. This allows us to start the healing process for not only ourselves but those around us as well.

By following these steps, owning up to our mistakes becomes less daunting and more achievable – leading us closer towards recovery and growth as individuals.

The Benefits of Admitting Our Wrongs

Acknowledging the harm we've caused can lead to improved relationships and a greater sense of self-awareness. One of the benefits of admitting our wrongs is that it allows us to take responsibility for our actions. When we own up to our mistakes, we show those around us that we're mature enough to face the consequences of our behavior.

This can help repair damaged relationships and build trust with others. Another benefit is that admitting our wrongs can bring us closer to understanding ourselves better. It takes courage and vulnerability to admit when we've done something wrong, but it also shows that we're willing to learn from our mistakes.

By being honest about where we went wrong, we can begin to identify patterns in our behavior and work towards becoming better versions of ourselves. Admitting our wrongs can also be an act of service towards others. When we acknowledge the harm we've caused someone else, it allows them space for healing and closure.

It shows that their feelings are valid and that their pain has been heard. Taking responsibility for our actions in this way is a small but important step towards making amends with those who've been hurt by us. Admitting our wrongs is an essential part of personal growth and spiritual development.

We can't evolve as individuals if we continue to deny or ignore the ways in which we've harmed others or ourselves. Admitting where we went wrong allows us space for reflection, forgiveness, and growth. It opens up new possibilities for how we relate with ourselves, others, and the world around us.

In conclusion, while admitting our wrongs may not always be easy or comfortable, there are many benefits that come along with doing so – both personally and socially. By taking responsibility for what we've done wrong, learning from these experiences, serving those who were affected by them, positively impacting human relationships development, being open-minded about what comes next, which ultimately leads to personal growth!

Making Amends and Moving Forward

It's time to make things right and move forward, even if it means swallowing our pride and asking for forgiveness. Let's show some heart and take the necessary steps to repair any damage that has been done.

Admitting our wrongs is a crucial step towards healing ourselves and others who may have been affected by our actions. This can be a difficult process because it involves facing the consequences of our actions. However, admitting to someone else the exact nature of our wrongs can bring relief from guilt and shame.

Once we've admitted our wrongs, it's important to ask for forgiveness from those we've hurt. This takes courage because there's no guarantee that they will forgive us or want anything to do with us again. But taking responsibility for our mistakes shows that we value their feelings and are willing to do whatever it takes to make things right.

Moving forward means making a commitment to change our behavior going forward. We can't undo what has already been done, but we can learn from our mistakes and strive to become better people each day. By continuing on this path of self-improvement, we can create positive change not just in ourselves but in those around us as well.

Maintaining Accountability and Responsibility

Maintaining accountability and responsibility means consistently owning up to our actions and making an effort to make things right. It's not enough to simply admit our wrongs in step five of the twelve-step program; we must continue to take responsibility for our behavior moving forward.

This includes staying aware of our actions and their impact on others, as well as taking steps to make amends for past mistakes. One important aspect of maintaining accountability is regularly checking in with ourselves about how we're doing. This can involve journaling, talking with a trusted friend or sponsor, or attending support group meetings.

By remaining vigilant about our thoughts and behaviors, we can catch ourselves before slipping back into old patterns that may have caused harm in the past. Another essential part of being accountable is making things right when we've done wrong.

This means following through on any promises we've made during the recovery process, whether it's apologizing to someone we've hurt or paying back money owed from previous debts. It also involves taking action to prevent future harm by setting healthy boundaries and avoiding situations where we're likely to act out.

Ultimately, maintaining accountability and responsibility is about living a life guided by principles such as honesty, integrity, compassion, and humility. By continually striving towards these ideals, even when it's difficult or uncomfortable, we create a better world not just for ourselves but for those around us as well.

As recovering addicts, this is one of the most rewarding aspects of the journey – knowing that by serving others and staying accountable for our actions, we're making a positive difference in the world.

Embracing a Life of Sobriety and Growth

By embracing a life of sobriety and growth, we can open ourselves up to new opportunities and experiences that were once unavailable to us. Living sober means breaking free from the chains of addiction and taking responsibility for our actions. It requires us to be honest with ourselves about who we are and what we've done wrong in the past.

When we admit our wrongdoings to God, ourselves, and another human being, it's a sign that we're willing to take ownership of our mistakes. We acknowledge that our actions have hurt others and that we want to make amends. This admission is an essential part of recovery because it helps us move forward by letting go of the shame and guilt that often accompany addiction.

Embracing sobriety also means making positive changes in our lives. We must work on building healthy relationships, finding new hobbies or interests, developing coping mechanisms for stress or anxiety, and seeking out support from others who understand what we're going through. By doing these things, we create a strong foundation for lasting recovery while serving as an example for others struggling with addiction.

Embracing a life of sobriety and growth is not just about avoiding drugs or alcohol; it's about creating a fulfilling existence built on honesty, accountability, and personal responsibility. When we admit our wrongs to God, ourselves, and another human being, we take an important step towards healing both ourselves and those around us. By living soberly each day with intentionality and purpose - even in small ways - we can serve as shining examples of hope for those still struggling with addiction.

Frequently Asked Questions

What are some common mistakes people make when choosing someone to confide in during Step Five?

When choosing someone to confide in during Step Five, common mistakes include picking someone who may judge or gossip about us. It's important to choose a trustworthy and non-judgmental person who can provide support and encouragement.

How can someone prepare themselves mentally and emotionally for the admission process?

To prepare ourselves for the admission process, we can start by acknowledging our mistakes and accepting responsibility for them. We can also seek guidance from a trusted mentor or counselor, and practice self-care to strengthen our emotional resilience.

What are some potential risks of not admitting our wrongs during Step Five?

Not admitting our wrongs during Step Five can lead to continued guilt and shame, further damaging relationships and hindering personal growth. It takes courage, but being honest with ourselves and others is a crucial step towards healing and restoration.

How can Step Five help individuals overcome their addiction and maintain sobriety in the long term?

Did you know that individuals who complete Step Five have a higher chance of maintaining sobriety long-term? By admitting our wrongs, we can address underlying issues and build accountability with others, leading to lasting recovery.

How does Step Five tie in with the overall 12-step program of recovery in AA?

Step five is a crucial part of the 12-step program. It involves admitting our wrongs to God, ourselves, and another person. This helps us take responsibility for our actions and make amends, leading to long-term sobriety.

Conclusion

In conclusion, Step Five of recovery is an essential part of our journey towards sobriety and growth. By admitting to God, ourselves, and another human being the exact nature of our wrongs, we confront and acknowledge our shortcomings.

It can be scary to admit our mistakes, but understanding the importance of this step helps us overcome that fear. Choosing the right person to confide in and making amends are crucial to moving forward with accountability and responsibility.

Just like a seed needs water and sunlight to grow into a plant, we need honesty and vulnerability to transform ourselves into better versions of who we were before. So let's embrace this step with open hearts and minds, knowing that by doing so we can create a life full of purpose and joy - just like a butterfly emerging from its cocoon.

STEP SIX

We Were Entirely Ready To Have God Remove All These Defects of Character

As we embark on the journey of recovery, we come to a point where we must confront our defects of character. It can be a daunting task to face these imperfections head-on, but it is essential for our growth and transformation.

Step Six in the 12 step program asks us to become entirely ready to have God remove all these defects of character. This step requires a willingness to let go of the things that are holding us back and embracing a new way of life.

Like pulling weeds from a garden, Step Six calls for us to acknowledge our flaws and work towards removing them completely. It requires humility and an open mind as we recognize that we cannot overcome these defects on our own. We must seek guidance from a higher power, whatever that may mean for each individual.

In this article, we will explore what it means to be entirely ready and how this step can lead us towards freedom from our shortcomings.

Understanding Step Six in the twelve steps of recovery

Now, we're ready to let go of our character flaws and allow a higher power to take control. Step Six in the program is all about being completely prepared for the removal of our defects of character.

This step requires us to be willing to give up our old ways of thinking and behaving that have caused us harm and pain in the past. We must understand that this step is not just about making a list of our faults but also being open and honest with ourselves about how these defects affect others around us.

It's important to remember that we aren't alone in this journey; we have support from other members who have gone through the same process. At this point, it's crucial to realize that we can't do this on our own; we need help from a higher power.

We must surrender ourselves entirely, trust that God will guide us on the right path, and have faith that He will remove all our defects of character. Once we let go, it becomes easier for us to focus on improving ourselves without worrying about controlling everything.

Step Six is an essential part of the twelve steps of recovery as it allows us to be willing and open-minded towards change. Being entirely ready means giving up control over things beyond our reach while having faith in a higher power's plan for us.

By taking this step seriously, we become more humble, self-aware individuals who are committed to serving others while working towards a better version of ourselves every day.

Acknowledging the Need for Help

Recognizing our imperfections and acknowledging that we need help can be a humbling yet empowering experience. In Step Six of the twelve steps of recovery, we come to terms with the fact that we are not perfect and are ready to have God remove our defects of character. This step is crucial in our journey towards recovery because it requires us to admit that we cannot do this alone.

It takes humility to admit that we have flaws. Many of us grew up believing that vulnerability was a sign of weakness, but in reality, it's quite the opposite. Acknowledging our weaknesses allows us to take control over them and work towards becoming better versions of ourselves. It also creates an opportunity for growth and self-discovery.

As we begin working on Step Six, we must remind ourselves that change doesn't happen overnight. It's a process that requires patience and persistence. We may feel discouraged or overwhelmed at times, but it's vital to remember why we started this journey in the first place - for a better life free from addiction.

Acknowledging the need for help is essential when working through Step Six of the twelve steps of recovery. It takes courage to face our imperfections head-on and accept help from others as well as ourselves. Remembering why we started this journey will keep us motivated during challenging times, while recognizing small victories along the way will bring us closer towards achieving long-term success in our recovery journey.

Defining the Concept of God in Step Six

Embracing the concept of a higher power, whether it's the universe, nature, or a traditional deity, is integral to Step Six. This step requires us to relinquish our ego and acknowledge that we can't overcome our flaws alone. By recognizing that there's something greater than ourselves at work in the universe, we open ourselves up to new possibilities and growth.

Here are four ways defining the concept of God can help us in Step Six:

- It allows us to release control. When we try to fix ourselves, we often feel overwhelmed and frustrated. Defining a higher power helps us realize that there are forces beyond our control in the world. By surrendering our will to this power, we can find peace and serenity.
- It gives us hope. Sometimes it's hard to believe that we can change for the better. But by trusting in a higher power's ability to help us remove our flaws, we can approach recovery with renewed hope and optimism.
- It reminds us that we're not alone. Many people feel isolated and disconnected when they first enter recovery. But by embracing a higher power, even if it's just the collective energy of humanity working toward good, we can feel like part of something larger than ourselves.
- It provides a moral compass. One common struggle among those recovering from addiction is figuring out how to live a meaningful life without drugs or alcohol. By defining the values our higher power embodies – honesty, compassion, love – we can use those principles as guidance for our actions moving forward.

Overall, defining what 'God' means to us is a vital part of Step Six in. It allows us to tap into something greater than ourselves while also finding direction and purpose on our journey towards recovery.

Letting Go of Defects of Character

It can be challenging to release the negative aspects of yourself that have become so ingrained, but letting go of these defects of character is crucial in your journey towards recovery.

In Step Six, we were entirely ready to have God remove all our shortcomings and character flaws. This step requires us to take a long, hard look at ourselves and identify our negative traits without judgment or self-criticism.

Once we've identified these defects of character, it's time to let them go. It's not enough to simply recognize them; we must actively work towards removing them from our lives. This process requires humility and surrender – we have to admit that there are things about ourselves that need changing, and trust that with God's help, we can make those changes.

The beauty of this step is that it allows us to shed the negativity that has been holding us back for so long. By letting go of our defects of character, we make room for positive change and growth in our lives.

We become more compassionate towards ourselves and others, more patient in difficult situations, and better able to handle life's challenges with grace and resilience.

Step Six is all about letting go – letting go of the things that no longer serve us so that we can make space for positive growth in our lives. It's not an easy process, but with God's help and the support of others on the same journey as us, it's possible. So let go of your shortcomings today – you'll be amazed at how much freer you feel once you do!

Being Willing to Change

You have to be willing to change if you want to overcome the obstacles that are holding you back and create a better future for yourself. This step of being entirely ready to have God remove all these defects of character is crucial in our journey towards recovery. It means we acknowledge and accept that there are parts of ourselves that need improvement, and we're open to letting go of them.

Being willing to change requires courage. It's not easy to confront our flaws and admit that we need help. But with willingness comes hope - hope for a brighter future, hope for a healthier relationship with ourselves and others, and hope for a fulfilling life.

Here are some ways we can cultivate this willingness:

- Be honest with yourself about your shortcomings.
- Practice self-reflection regularly.
- Seek feedback from trusted sources.
- Embrace discomfort as an opportunity for growth.
- Stay committed to the process, even when it gets tough.

As we embark on this journey towards becoming the best version of ourselves, it's important to remember that change doesn't happen overnight. It's a gradual process that requires patience, persistence, and compassion towards oneself. We must also trust in our higher power or whatever source of strength we believe in; knowing that they will guide us through every step of the way.

Being entirely ready to have God remove all these defects of character means recognizing our flaws and having the courage to let go of them. It takes time, effort, and commitment but by cultivating willingness through honesty, self-reflection, seeking feedback, embracing discomforts as opportunities for growth while trusting our higher power or source; we can achieve true transformation within ourselves which ultimately leads us on a path serving others' needs along with ours as well.

Examining Personal Shortcomings

By taking a closer look at our personal flaws, we can uncover areas where we may be holding ourselves back from achieving our full potential. This is why in step six of the twelve-step program, we were entirely ready to have God remove all these defects of character. It's important to remember that this doesn't mean we'll suddenly become perfect human beings, but rather that we're willing to do the work necessary to address and improve upon our shortcomings.

Examining our personal flaws can feel uncomfortable or even painful at times, but it's an essential part of growth and self-improvement. We must be honest with ourselves about areas in which we struggle or fall short if we want to make meaningful changes. This process requires humility and vulnerability, as it means admitting that we don't have everything figured out and need help from a higher power.

It's also crucial to recognize that personal growth isn't just for our benefit; when we overcome our character defects, it allows us to better serve others. By acknowledging and addressing our shortcomings, we become better equipped to show up fully for those around us and make a positive impact on their lives.

By being entirely ready to have God remove all these defects of character in step six of the twelve-step program, we commit ourselves to examining personal flaws honestly and humbly. While this process can be challenging at times, it ultimately leads us towards greater self-awareness and the ability to serve others more effectively.

Seeking Transformation and Growth

Let's explore how seeking transformation and growth can lead us towards becoming the best version of ourselves. As we move forward in our recovery journey, it's important to remember that we're not perfect and there'll always be areas where we need improvement. However, by acknowledging our shortcomings and taking action to correct them, we can begin to transform into the person we aspire to be.

The first step in seeking transformation and growth is being willing to change. This means setting aside our ego and accepting that we don't have all the answers. It takes courage to admit when we're wrong or when our behavior is hurting those around us. By doing so, however, we open ourselves up to growth and new possibilities.

Another key aspect of seeking transformation is being open-minded. We must be willing to consider new ideas and perspectives, even if they challenge our current beliefs or ways of thinking. This doesn't mean abandoning our values or principles, but rather expanding our understanding of the world around us.

Finally, seeking transformation requires a willingness to take action towards positive change. It's not enough to simply acknowledge our flaws; we must actively work towards improving ourselves every day through intentional actions and behaviors.

By embracing these principles of willingness, open-mindedness, and action-oriented thinking, we can begin the process of transforming ourselves into better people who are more capable of serving others with love and compassion. Let's continue on this path towards self-improvement with humility and grace as we strive towards becoming the best version of ourselves possible.

Overcoming Obstacles in the Process

Overcoming obstacles in the process can be challenging, but it's important to remember that setbacks are a natural part of growth and transformation.

As we work towards being entirely ready to have God remove all our defects of character, there may be times when we stumble. Perhaps we struggle with anger management or find it difficult to forgive others. These habits may have been ingrained in us for years, making them hard to break.

However, it's important not to give up hope. When faced with an obstacle, we must remind ourselves of our commitment and continue moving forward. We can take inspiration from those who have overcome similar challenges before us and seek support from loved ones or professional guidance if needed.

Another way to overcome obstacles is by practicing self-care. This involves taking care of our physical, emotional, and spiritual needs so that we can better manage stressors as they arise. Some people find solace in prayer or meditation while others enjoy exercise or spending time outdoors.

Overcoming obstacles on the path towards being entirely ready for transformation requires patience, persistence, and self-compassion. We must acknowledge that setbacks will happen but use them as opportunities for growth instead of letting them discourage us from moving forward.

With dedication and a willingness to change, we can become the best versions of ourselves and serve others with love and compassion along the way.

Finding Support in the Fellowship

You can find immense support and guidance from the fellowship as you navigate through your journey towards becoming the best version of yourself. It's essential to surround ourselves with like-minded individuals who share our goals and aspirations.

In step six, we acknowledge that we're not perfect and have defects of character that need to be removed. However, this process requires a lot of effort and work, which can be challenging to do on our own.

By joining a fellowship, we open ourselves up to a community where we can receive emotional support from people who understand what we're going through. We no longer feel alone in our struggles, and it becomes easier to share our fears and insecurities with others without any judgment or criticism.

Attending meetings allows us to learn from other people's experiences and gain insight into how they overcame their obstacles. This knowledge helps us identify the areas where we need improvement and develop strategies for tackling them.

Moreover, participating in group activities such as service projects or social events provides an opportunity for us to give back while also building meaningful relationships with others who share similar values. This sense of belonging brings joy and fulfillment into our lives while fostering personal growth.

Finding support in the fellowship is crucial for anyone looking to overcome their defects of character actively. By surrounding ourselves with like-minded individuals who understand what we're going through, attending meetings regularly, learning from other people's experiences, participating in group activities such as service projects or social events- all these things help us stay accountable during tough times while fostering personal growth along the way.

Remember: You don't have to go through your journey alone – reach out today!

Embracing a New Way of Life

Embracing a new way of life can be challenging, but it's also an opportunity for growth and transformation. As we progress through our recovery journey, we learn that the defects of character that once held us back are no longer serving us.

It takes courage to acknowledge these flaws and to take responsibility for changing them. However, the rewards are immeasurable. Having a willingness to change is crucial in this step. We must accept that our old ways of thinking and behaving were not working for us and be open to a new way of living.

This can mean letting go of old habits, relationships, and beliefs that no longer serve us. It can be intimidating at first, but with support from our higher power and community, we can move forward with confidence.

As we embrace this new way of life, we begin to see positive changes in ourselves and our relationships with others. We start living authentically instead of trying to please others or hide behind masks. Our interactions become more genuine as we let go of manipulative behaviors or defensive attitudes.

By working on ourselves, we inspire others to do the same. Embracing a new way of life is a vital step towards lasting recovery and personal growth. Although it may feel daunting at first, having faith in ourselves and our higher power will help guide us through this transformative process.

Remembering that our efforts will not only benefit ourselves but also those around us helps motivate us towards continued progress on this journey called life.

Frequently Asked Questions

What is the history of Step Six in the twelve steps of recovery?

Step Six in the program has evolved over time, but it has always focused on becoming ready for God to remove our character defects. This step helps us continue our journey towards a fulfilling life of service to others.

How do other recovery programs approach the concept of Step Six?

Other recovery programs approach Step Six similarly to AA, emphasizing the need for self-awareness and willingness to change. We recognize the importance of surrendering character defects to a higher power and embracing personal growth as a means of serving others in recovery.

Can Step Six be completed without belief in a higher power?

Studies show that 64% of people in recovery struggle with the concept of a higher power. While Step Six involves being ready for change, it can still be completed without belief in God. It's about acknowledging our flaws and being willing to work on them for the benefit of ourselves and others.

How long does it typically take to be "entirely ready" for Step Six?

It varies for each person, but we work towards being entirely ready by acknowledging our defects of character and actively seeking to change them. It's a continuous process of self-reflection and growth, guided by personal values and principles.

Are there any specific techniques or practices recommended for letting go of defects of character?

To let go of defects of character, we can practice mindfulness, self-reflection, and asking for guidance from a higher power. It's important to be willing and open to change, and to continue working towards growth and improvement.

Conclusion

So there we were, standing at the threshold of Step Six, entirely ready to have God remove all these defects of character. It was a moment of surrender, a recognition that our own efforts had been insufficient and that we needed help beyond ourselves.

But it was also a moment of hope, an acknowledgment that transformation and growth were possible if we were willing to do the work. As we moved forward in this step, we let go of the things that had held us back for so long: fear, resentment, selfishness, and more.

We opened ourselves up to change and accepted the challenge to become better versions of ourselves. And while there were certainly obstacles along the way - moments when old habits threatened to resurface or when doubts crept in - we found support in each other and in our shared commitment to recovery.

In conclusion, as we stood on the other side of Step Six, looking back at how far we had come, we realized that this journey was about much more than just getting rid of defects. It was about embracing a new way of life - one rooted in humility, authenticity, and service.

It wasn't always easy or comfortable but it was worth it because it allowed us to live with purpose and meaning. As they say, "life is a journey not a destination"and with each step on this path towards spiritual growth and freedom from addiction; we are reminded that every obstacle can be overcome with persistence towards our goal!

STEP SEVEN

We Humbly Asked Him to Remove Our Shortcomings

As we continue our journey through the twelve steps of recovery, we come to step seven: "We humbly asked Him to remove our shortcomings."

This step is one of surrender and humility, as we acknowledge that we are not perfect and that we cannot overcome our struggles on our own. It requires us to trust in a higher power and let go of ego and pride in order to achieve lasting growth and transformation.

Step seven is a crucial step in the recovery process because it allows us to confront our character defects and work towards overcoming them. By acknowledging our shortcomings, embracing humility, and seeking help from a higher power, we can make positive changes in our lives and cultivate self-awareness.

Ultimately, this step leads us towards a life of service to others, as we become more compassionate, understanding, and empathetic towards those around us. Join me as we explore the importance of Step Seven in recovery.

Understanding the Importance of Step Seven in Recovery

Now, you're probably wondering why Step Seven is such a crucial part of your recovery journey. Well, let me tell you that this step is where we start to see the real change in ourselves.

Step Seven requires us to humbly ask our higher power to remove our shortcomings, and this act of surrender helps us grow spiritually and emotionally.

One of the key reasons why Step Seven is so important is because it helps us let go of our ego and pride. When we admit that we have flaws and actively seek help in overcoming them, we become more open-minded and accepting of feedback from others. This humility allows us to rebuild relationships that may have been damaged by our addiction.

Furthermore, Step Seven encourages us to take responsibility for our actions. We realize that we are not perfect beings and that there are certain things about ourselves that need improvement. By asking our higher power for help in removing these shortcomings, we acknowledge that we cannot do it alone and need guidance from something greater than ourselves.

Lastly, Step Seven teaches us how to be patient with ourselves as we work towards becoming better people. It's easy to get frustrated when progress seems slow or when setbacks occur, but by humbly asking for help every day, we learn how to trust the process and have faith in something beyond what we can see or control.

I believe that Step Seven is an essential component of any successful recovery journey. Through humility, acceptance of feedback from others, taking responsibility for our actions, and learning patience with ourselves – all while seeking guidance from a higher power – we can overcome even the most challenging obstacles on the path towards healing.

Acknowledging Our Shortcomings

As you come to terms with your imperfections and flaws, you must confront them head-on and take ownership of them. Admitting our shortcomings is a crucial step in the recovery process as it allows us to identify areas where we need improvement. We can't change what we don't acknowledge, so it's essential to be honest with ourselves about our weaknesses.

To fully understand our shortcomings, we must first identify them. This can be done by asking ourselves tough questions such as: What are my character defects? Where have I fallen short in my relationships or responsibilities? What habits or behaviors do I need to change?

Once we have identified these areas, it becomes easier to ask for help from a higher power or seek guidance from others who have gone through similar experiences.

Once we have acknowledged our shortcomings, the next step is to humbly ask a higher power to remove them. This requires surrendering control and relying on something greater than ourselves for help. It also means being open-minded and willing to accept solutions that may not align with our initial thoughts or beliefs.

Acknowledging our shortcomings is an important part of the recovery process. It requires honesty, introspection, and humility, but ultimately leads us towards growth and self-improvement. By identifying areas of weakness and asking for help from a higher power or support network, we can overcome these challenges and become better versions of ourselves.

Embracing Humility in the Recovery Process

Embracing humility allows us to accept the reality of our imperfections and become receptive to change throughout the recovery process. It takes courage to acknowledge our shortcomings and ask for help in addressing them.

Humility is essential in this process, as it helps us recognize that we cannot do it alone. We need the support of others, including a higher power, to overcome our weaknesses.

Humility also means recognizing our limitations and being willing to learn from others. It involves setting aside our ego and being open-minded about new ideas or ways of doing things. This can be challenging at times, especially when we're used to being in control or thinking that we know best.

However, by embracing humility, we become teachable and more willing to listen to the guidance of those around us.

In recovery, humility is vital because it helps us stay grounded and focused on what truly matters. Instead of getting caught up in our own desires or expectations, we learn how to be present in the moment and appreciate the blessings that come with sobriety.

By staying humble, we avoid becoming complacent or overconfident in our progress. Embracing humility is an essential part of the recovery journey. It allows us to accept ourselves as imperfect human beings who need help from others along the way.

By cultivating a humble attitude towards life and sobriety, we can continue growing and evolving into better versions of ourselves each day.

Trusting in a Higher Power

Trusting in a higher power can provide a sense of peace and guidance throughout the recovery process. It's essential to recognize that we can't overcome our shortcomings on our own.

We need to rely on something greater than ourselves, whether it's God or another spiritual entity. By acknowledging this, we're taking the first step towards humility and surrendering control.

Asking a higher power to remove our shortcomings is an act of faith and trust. We must let go of our ego and accept that we're not perfect beings. We all have flaws and imperfections, but it's through recognizing them that we can work towards becoming better versions of ourselves. This requires vulnerability, honesty, and a willingness to change.

Trusting in a higher power also means letting go of past resentments and forgiving those who have wronged us. Holding onto grudges only creates more pain and suffering within ourselves. By releasing these negative emotions, we open up space for love, compassion, and inner peace.

Trusting in a higher power is essential for anyone on the path towards recovery. It allows us to let go of control, embrace humility, and find peace within ourselves. Through this process of surrendering to something greater than ourselves, we can begin to heal from our past mistakes and move forward with hope for the future.

Letting Go of Ego and Pride

Letting go of ego and pride is crucial for achieving long-term recovery, as it allows us to focus on our personal growth rather than protecting our self-image. Admitting that we have shortcomings and asking a Higher Power to remove them can be difficult, especially if we've spent years trying to hide our flaws from others. However, by acknowledging our imperfections, we allow ourselves to become more vulnerable and open to change.

One way to let go of ego and pride is to practice humility. This involves recognizing that we're not perfect and that everyone makes mistakes. By accepting this fact, we can begin to let go of the need for control and perfection in every aspect of our lives.

Humility also means being willing to learn from others and seek guidance when needed. Another helpful tool in letting go of ego and pride is practicing gratitude. When we focus on what we're grateful for rather than what's lacking in our lives, it becomes easier to let go of feelings of entitlement or superiority.

Gratitude also helps us maintain perspective on what's truly important in life. Developing empathy towards others can also help us let go of ego and pride. By putting ourselves in someone else's shoes, we gain a deeper understanding of their struggles and limitations.

This can help us become more patient with ourselves as well as with those around us. In conclusion, letting go of ego and pride is an essential step towards achieving long-term recovery. It requires a willingness to admit our imperfections, practice humility, gratitude, and empathy towards others while focusing on personal growth over self-image protection.

By doing so, we create space for positive change in ourselves while serving as inspirations for others seeking similar transformations along their road toward recovery.

Seeking Help and Support

As we continue our journey towards recovery, we must acknowledge that letting go of ego and pride isn't enough. We must also seek help and support from a higher power. This is where step seven comes in - "we humbly asked Him to remove our shortcomings."

At this stage, we recognize that we can't conquer our shortcomings on our own. We need the guidance and assistance of a higher power to overcome them. It takes humility to admit that we're not invincible and can't do everything ourselves.

Asking for help can be difficult, especially when it comes to something as personal as our shortcomings. However, by asking for help, we open ourselves up to receive the support and guidance necessary for progress.

When we're humble enough to ask for help, it shows strength rather than weakness.

It's important to remember that seeking help doesn't mean we're weak or incapable of handling our problems alone. It simply means that we understand the value of community and recognize the innate desire within us all to serve others.

By asking for help with humility and grace, we allow others to fulfill their own desires for service while simultaneously allowing ourselves the opportunity for growth and healing.

Step seven is an essential part of the recovery process as it allows us to seek help and support in conquering our shortcomings through humility and grace. By acknowledging that overcoming these flaws can't be achieved alone, but only with divine intervention or spiritual principles guiding us towards success; it opens doors for growth opportunities within oneself while providing a fulfilling sense of purpose through serving others who may have similar struggles as well!

Overcoming Character Defects

Overcoming our character defects requires us to confront the uncomfortable parts of ourselves head-on and work towards growth with a willingness to change. We must acknowledge our flaws and be open to receiving help from others, whether it's through therapy, support groups, or guidance from trusted friends.

It takes humility to admit that we have shortcomings, but it's necessary in order for us to move forward on our path of self-improvement. As we ask a higher power to remove our shortcomings, we're also taking responsibility for our actions and their impact on those around us. We can't control the behavior of others, but we can control how we react and interact with them.

By working on ourselves and seeking to become better individuals, we can positively influence those around us and create a ripple effect of kindness and compassion. In this process of overcoming character defects, it's important that we don't fall into the trap of perfectionism. We'll make mistakes along the way, but what matters most is that we continue striving towards growth and improvement.

It takes time and effort to break old patterns and establish new ones, but with persistence comes progress. Ultimately, by humbly asking for help in removing our shortcomings, we're opening ourselves up to a world of possibilities. We're acknowledging that there's always room for growth and improvement in every aspect of our lives.

Through this process of self-discovery, we can become better versions of ourselves not just for ourselves, but also for those around us who may benefit from our positive transformation.

Cultivating Self-Awareness

By peering inward to understand our deepest desires and motivations, we can gain a greater sense of self-awareness and unlock the potential for personal growth. This process involves identifying our character defects and acknowledging their impact on ourselves and those around us. It requires humility and a willingness to face uncomfortable truths about ourselves.

Through self-reflection, we can begin to recognize patterns in our behavior that stem from underlying fears, insecurities, or past traumas. By becoming more aware of how these issues manifest in our daily lives, we can start taking steps towards addressing them. This may involve seeking therapy or counseling, practicing mindfulness techniques like meditation or journaling, or simply making a conscious effort to act differently in situations where we would normally react negatively.

Cultivating self-awareness is an ongoing practice that requires patience and persistence. It's not always easy to confront our flaws or admit when we're wrong, but by doing so we open ourselves up to new opportunities for growth and transformation.

When we are able to let go of our ego-driven desires and focus instead on serving others, we become more compassionate and empathetic individuals who are better equipped to navigate the challenges of life with grace and humility.

Asking God (or your higher power) to remove our shortcomings is an important step in the recovery process. But it's only through cultivating self-awareness that we can truly understand what those shortcomings are and work towards overcoming them. By committing ourselves to this ongoing practice of introspection and personal development, we can become the best versions of ourselves – not just for our own sake but for the benefit of those around us as well.

Making Positive Changes in Our Lives

You can start making positive changes in your life by identifying areas where you want to grow and taking small steps towards improvement. It's important to be honest with yourself and acknowledge the areas where you fall short, whether it's a bad habit or a character flaw. Once you've identified these shortcomings, it's time to take action.

One way to address our shortcomings is by asking for help from a higher power. In step seven of the 12-step program, we humbly ask our higher power to remove our defects of character. This requires us to let go of our ego and admit that we cannot overcome these flaws on our own. By surrendering control and trusting in something greater than ourselves, we open ourselves up to healing and transformation.

Another important aspect of making positive changes in our lives is accountability. We need people around us who will hold us accountable for our actions and encourage us along the way. Whether it's a sponsor in the 12-step program or simply a trusted friend or family member, having someone who cares about our growth can make all the difference.

Cultivating gratitude is essential in making positive changes in our lives. When we focus on what we're grateful for rather than dwelling on what we lack, we create an abundance mindset that fuels positivity and growth. By acknowledging all the good things in our lives, even amidst challenges and struggles, we gain perspective and resilience that helps us navigate life with grace and humility.

Achieving Lasting Growth and Transformation

As we continue on our journey towards making positive changes in our lives, one of the most important steps is to humbly ask for help in removing our shortcomings. This step requires us to be honest with ourselves and acknowledge that we're not perfect, that there are things about us that need improvement. It takes humility to admit this, but it's necessary for achieving lasting growth and transformation.

When we humbly ask for help in removing our shortcomings, we're acknowledging that we can't do it alone. We need the help of a higher power, whether it be God or some other spiritual force.

This act of surrendering control can be difficult for some, but it's essential if we want to experience true change in our lives.

Achieving lasting growth and transformation requires perseverance and dedication. It takes time and effort to overcome our shortcomings and become the best version of ourselves.

But by taking this step towards humility and asking for help, we're setting ourselves up for success. We're showing a willingness to learn from others and make the necessary changes to improve ourselves.

By humbly asking for help in removing our shortcomings, we're taking an important step towards achieving lasting growth and transformation.

It may not always be easy or comfortable, but it's necessary if we want to live fulfilling lives filled with purpose and meaning.

So let's embrace this step with an open heart and mind, knowing that when we surrender control and ask for help from a higher power, great things can happen.

Markdown list:

1. Acknowledge imperfections
2. Surrender control
3. Persevere through difficulties

Frequently Asked Questions

What are some common shortcomings that people ask to have removed in Step Seven?

In Step Seven, we ask for our shortcomings to be removed. Common ones include selfishness, anger, and fear. We're willing to let go of these defects so we can better serve others and live a more fulfilling life.

How is Step Seven different from other steps in the recovery process?

Step Seven is unique because it requires humility and surrendering our shortcomings to a higher power. It's not just about identifying our flaws, but actively seeking help in overcoming them. This process allows us to grow and serve others better.

Can Step Seven be completed without belief in a higher power?

Yes, Step Seven can be completed without belief in a higher power. We recognize our shortcomings and commit to improving ourselves with the help of support systems and introspection. It's about taking responsibility for our actions and striving for personal growth.

What are some strategies for staying humble during the recovery process?

Staying humble in recovery can be challenging. We focus on helping others, practicing self-reflection, and accepting feedback. Euphemistically speaking, we see our shortcomings as opportunities for growth and ask a higher power (if applicable) to guide us towards progress.

How can individuals know if they have successfully completed Step Seven?

We know we've completed Step Seven when we experience a sense of relief and freedom from our shortcomings. We feel empowered to serve others and are open to continued growth. It's an ongoing process, but one that brings us closer to our higher power.

Conclusion

In conclusion, Step Seven has been crucial in our journey towards recovery. It's helped us acknowledge our shortcomings and embrace humility as a key component of the process. By trusting in a higher power, we've been able to let go of ego and pride. This allows us to overcome our character defects.

Through this step, we've cultivated self-awareness and made positive changes in our lives. This has resulted in lasting growth and transformation. We never thought it was possible before.

Step Seven is like a seed that's grown into a beautiful flower. It represents the beauty that comes from facing our flaws head-on and working towards becoming better versions of ourselves every day.

STEP EIGHT

We Made A List of All Persons We Had Harmed and Became Willing To Make Amends to Them All

This step is one of the key components of the twelve steps of recovery, which guide participants through a process of self-examination and spiritual growth. Step Eight – "We made a list of all persons we had harmed and became willing to make amends to them all" – is a pivotal point on this journey.

Step Eight requires us to confront our past mistakes and take responsibility for our actions. It's not an easy task, but it's necessary for personal growth and healing. By making a comprehensive list of people we have harmed, we can examine the impact our actions have had on others.

This step also demonstrates our commitment to change and willingness to make things right. Making amends can be challenging, but with guidance from supportive individuals and the power of forgiveness, it's possible to find peace and move forward in life.

In this article, we will explore Step Eight more deeply and provide insight into how it can help us serve others as well as ourselves.

Understanding the Purpose of Step Eight in Recovery

Now we'll explore why Step Eight is an essential part of the twelve steps of recovery. The purpose of this step is to help us identify all the people we have wronged in our past and become willing to make amends with them.

This step enables us to take responsibility for our actions and seek forgiveness from those we've harmed. Making a list of all persons we've harmed might seem overwhelming, but it's crucial for our recovery process.

We must be honest with ourselves about the harm that was caused by our actions, whether it was intentional or unintentional. Identifying these individuals and their feelings helps us understand the impact of our behavior on others.

It's important to note that becoming willing to make amends does not necessarily mean that we will automatically correct every wrong that was done in the past. There may be situations where making amends would cause more harm than good, or where it isn't possible due to circumstances beyond our control.

In those cases, being willing means taking steps towards righting any wrongdoing as best as we can. Step Eight plays a critical role in helping us acknowledge and take responsibility for any harm we've caused others.

It allows us to grow emotionally and spiritually by seeking forgiveness from those who were affected by our behavior. By doing so, we can start repairing relationships and building a positive future free from guilt and shame.

Confronting Past Mistakes and Taking Responsibility

Taking responsibility for our past mistakes involves confronting them head-on and acknowledging the harm we may have caused. This requires us to look back at our past and identify all the people we have wronged. It's not an easy task, but it's necessary if we want to move forward in our recovery.

Once we have made a list of all the people we have harmed, step eight asks us to become willing to make amends to them all. This means that we need to be open-minded and willing to accept any consequences that may come from our actions. We can't control how others will react, but what we can control is our willingness to take responsibility for our actions.

Making amends is not just about saying sorry; it also involves making things right with those whom we have harmed. Sometimes this means making financial restitution or doing something specific for the person who was hurt. Whatever it takes, we need to be willing and committed to making things right so that both parties can move on from the situation.

Step eight is a crucial step in the recovery process. It allows us to confront our past mistakes and take responsibility for them. By making a list of all persons we had harmed and becoming willing to make amends, we are taking an active role in repairing relationships and healing ourselves. It's not always an easy road, but with commitment and dedication, anyone can overcome their past mistakes and move towards a brighter future filled with hope, forgiveness, and love.

Making a Comprehensive List of People Harmed

Start by putting yourself in the shoes of those you've wronged and imagine how they may have felt as a result of your actions. This is an important step towards making amends with them. You need to understand the gravity of your mistakes, acknowledge the pain you caused, and show genuine remorse for your actions.

Making a comprehensive list of people who were harmed gives you an opportunity to take responsibility for what you did and begin the process of repairing relationships. As you make this list, it's essential to be honest with yourself about who was affected by your behavior. It can be challenging to admit that we hurt others, but being truthful is crucial if we want to make things right.

Once you've identified everyone who was impacted by your actions, think about how each person might have felt. Consider their emotions, reactions, and possible consequences they faced because of what happened.

To make this process more manageable, try breaking down your list into three sub-lists:

1) Direct harm: These are people whom we directly wronged through our own actions or words. Examples include cheating on a partner or lying to a friend. In these cases, we need to reach out personally and apologize for our behavior.

2) Indirect harm: These are people who were affected by our actions even though they weren't necessarily targeted directly. For example, if we caused someone else distress which then had ripple effects onto another person - they would fall under indirect harm category. In such cases where direct communication isn't possible or appropriate (such as when someone has passed away), writing a letter can be helpful.

3) Systemic harm: These are harms that could happen due to larger societal issues such as racism or

sexism, etc. While it may not be feasible for us as individuals to directly apologize in these scenarios, seeking ways where one can reverse or repair some damage done through donating time/money, etc. can still help create positive change in the long run.

Making amends can be a difficult process. However, it's essential for our own healing and growth as well as the healing of those we have wronged. By creating a comprehensive list of people harmed, you're taking an important step towards making things right. Remember that this isn't about absolving ourselves of guilt but rather accepting responsibility for our actions. Through sincere apologies and genuine efforts to make amends, we can begin to rebuild relationships and live in harmony with others around us.

Examining the Impact of Actions on Others

To fully understand the impact of our actions on others, we need to take a step back and think about how they may have felt as a result of what we did. This requires us to put ourselves in their shoes and consider the emotions that were triggered by our behavior. It's not always easy to do this, especially when we're caught up in our own perspective, but it is vital if we want to make amends and repair damaged relationships.

When we examine the impact of our actions on others, it's important not just to focus on the immediate consequences but also on the long-term effects. For example, if you lied to someone or betrayed their trust, they may have lost faith in you and find it hard to trust anyone else again. They might feel hurt, angry, or even resentful towards you for a long time afterward.

By acknowledging this impact and taking responsibility for your actions, you can begin to repair the damage done.

Another aspect of examining the impact of our actions on others is recognizing patterns in our behavior that might be causing harm repeatedly. Maybe you tend to lash out at people when you're stressed or anxious, or maybe you have a habit of making promises that you can't keep. By identifying these patterns and becoming aware of how they affect those around us, we can work towards changing them and avoiding future harm.

Examining the impact of our actions on others is an essential part of making amends and repairing damaged relationships. It requires us to step outside ourselves and consider how other people are affected by what we do. By putting ourselves in their shoes and being willing to take responsibility for any harm caused, we can begin the process of healing both ourselves and those around us.

Demonstrating Commitment to Change

By committing to change, we can show those around us that we care about their feelings and are dedicated to making things right. It takes courage and humility to admit our wrongdoings, but it's an essential step towards healing relationships with the people we have harmed.

Making a list of all persons we've harmed isn't easy, but it's necessary for us to understand the impact of our actions on others. To demonstrate our commitment to change, we must be willing to make amends to everyone on that list.

This means taking responsibility for our past behaviors and actively seeking ways to make things right. It may involve apologizing in person or providing restitution for any damages caused by our actions. We can't force anyone to forgive us, but by showing genuine remorse and making a sincere effort to improve ourselves, we can begin the process of rebuilding trust.

Making amends also requires us to listen actively and empathetically when others express their hurt or anger towards us. We need to validate their feelings without becoming defensive or dismissive of their experiences. By doing so, we're acknowledging the harm that has been done and taking steps towards repairing the relationship.

Committing ourselves fully to making amends demonstrates our desire for growth and willingness to serve others. By acknowledging our past mistakes and working towards reconciliation with those we've harmed, we can begin the journey towards healing both ourselves and others.

Though difficult at times, this process ultimately leads us down a path of personal development where empathy and compassion take center stage in how we interact with those around us.

Seeking Forgiveness and Making Restitution

When you seek forgiveness and make restitution, it shows that you value the relationship and are willing to take action to repair any harm caused.

It's important to recognize that when we harm someone else, it not only affects them but also our own integrity. By acknowledging the harm we've caused, we can begin to repair the damage done and move forward with a clear conscience.

Making amends requires us to be willing to face difficult conversations and take responsibility for our actions. This may involve apologizing for hurtful words or actions, returning stolen property or giving back what was taken in some other way. It means taking positive steps towards repairing the relationship by showing genuine remorse.

The process of making amends isn't just about righting wrongs or restoring relationships - it's an opportunity for growth and self-reflection. It gives us a chance to examine our behavior and identify patterns that may have led us down this path in the first place. We must be open-minded, honest, and willing to learn from our mistakes if we want true transformation.

Seeking forgiveness and making restitution is an essential step towards healing ourselves and others. When we're able to acknowledge our mistakes and take action towards repairing them, we demonstrate our commitment not only to personal growth but also serving those around us.

The road ahead may be difficult but by taking this step, we'll find a renewed sense of purpose in life as well as deeper connections with those whom we've harmed along the way.

Identifying Practical Ways to Make Amends

You might be feeling overwhelmed by the thought of making amends, but remember that there are practical ways to approach this process that can make it more manageable.

The first step in identifying practical ways to make amends is to create a list of all the persons we've harmed. This list should include everyone, even those who we may have hurt unintentionally or indirectly.

Once we've identified these individuals, we need to reflect on the specific harm caused and how it impacted their lives. Next, we must become willing to make amends to them all. This means being open to feedback and criticism from those we've harmed and taking responsibility for our actions.

Sometimes making amends may involve apologizing directly to the person, while other times it may require us to take action that will benefit them or their community. It's important to keep in mind that making amends is not just about 'fixing' what was broken; it's about moving forward with integrity and building stronger relationships with those around us.

By taking concrete steps towards making things right, we demonstrate our commitment to growth and personal development. Identifying practical ways to make amends requires us to be honest with ourselves about the harm we've caused and willing to take steps towards healing and reconciliation.

Though it can be an uncomfortable process at times, ultimately it leads us towards greater personal growth and stronger connections with others. Remember: every small act of kindness or generosity has the potential for a ripple effect that can touch countless lives!

Overcoming Challenges in Making Amends

Making amends can be a difficult process, especially when we face challenges such as fear of rejection or uncertainty about how to approach the situation. It takes courage and humility to admit our wrongdoings and make things right with those we have hurt. However, there are ways to overcome these challenges and make the process of making amends easier.

1. Practice self-compassion: We often beat ourselves up over past mistakes, which can cause us to feel even more afraid of approaching those we have harmed. Practicing self-compassion means acknowledging that we all make mistakes and treating ourselves with kindness and understanding. By doing so, we can approach the situation with a clearer mind and heart.
2. Seek support from others: Making amends is not something that we have to do alone. It can be helpful to seek support from trusted friends or family members who can offer guidance and encouragement along the way. This also reminds us that we are not defined by our past mistakes but by our willingness to take responsibility for them.
3. Be sincere in your apology: When making amends, it's important to be sincere in your apology rather than just going through the motions. Take time to reflect on your actions and words before approaching the person you have harmed, so that you can convey genuine remorse for what you've done wrong.

Making amends is an essential step in recovery that requires courage, humility, and compassion towards oneself and others. While it may be a challenging process filled with fears of rejection or uncertainty about how best to approach the situation, there are practical steps one can take like practicing self-compassion, seeking support from others, being sincere in their apologies which will help overcome these hurdles for serving others better. Remembering that at its core this step is about taking responsibility for one's actions helps build resilience during this journey towards deeper personal transformation.

Finding Support and Guidance in the Process

Finding support and guidance in the process of making amends can be daunting, but reaching out for help can make it more manageable. By confiding in trusted friends or seeking professional therapy, we can gain the courage and strength needed to take responsibility for our actions.

It's important to remember that making amends is about taking ownership of our behavior and repairing any damage caused, not seeking forgiveness. A therapist can offer invaluable insight and emotional support in navigating these conversations. Surrounding ourselves with supportive friends and loved ones can also provide practical advice and a space for self-reflection.

Ultimately, finding support throughout the process is critical for achieving true healing and reconciliation. Having someone there every step of the way helps us stay accountable while providing the encouragement needed to keep moving forward. When making amends feels like navigating a dark forest without a map, having someone holding a flashlight makes all the difference in finding our way towards peace and resolution.

Celebrating Healing and Recovery through Step Eight

Celebrating the progress made in healing and recovery can be a rewarding experience, as we acknowledge the positive changes that have taken place in our lives. Step Eight is an important part of this process, as it allows us to reflect on the people we have harmed along the way.

It's easy to focus solely on our own journey, but making amends with those we've hurt is crucial for our continued growth and well-being. At first, making a list of all persons we had harmed may seem daunting or overwhelming. But as we go through this step, we begin to see how much power there is in taking responsibility for our actions and seeking forgiveness from others.

We become willing to make amends not because it's easy or comfortable, but because it's necessary for our own healing and for repairing relationships that may have been damaged along the way. As we work through Step Eight, it's important to remember that this isn't just about apologizing and moving on - it's about truly making things right.

This means being willing to listen to others' perspectives and feelings about what happened, taking ownership of our mistakes, and doing what we can to make things better. It may not always be possible to fully repair every relationship or situation, but the act of trying can bring a sense of closure and peace.

Ultimately, Step Eight serves as a reminder that recovery isn't just about abstaining from harmful behaviors - it's also about actively working towards becoming better people who are accountable for their actions. By acknowledging those we've wronged and taking steps towards making things right with them, we continue down the path of healing and growth while also serving others by showing them respect and kindness.

Frequently Asked Questions

How long does it typically take to complete Step Eight?

Completing Step Eight can vary in length depending on the individual and their situation. It requires a willingness to make amends with those we have harmed, which may take time to develop. However, our desire for serving others drives us to complete this step as thoroughly and promptly as possible.

What if someone on the list has passed away or is unreachable?

If someone on our Step Eight list has passed away or is unreachable, we can still make amends by finding alternative ways to show our willingness to make things right. We can donate to their favorite charity or write a letter of apology and burn it as a symbolic gesture.

Can making amends worsen a situation or cause harm to myself or others?

Making amends can be challenging, but it's worth it. It's important to approach the situation with humility and a willingness to listen. While it may not always lead to a positive outcome, taking responsibility for our actions can bring us peace and help repair damaged relationships.

How do I know if I am truly ready and willing to make amends?

So you think you're ready to make amends, eh? Well, first off, put your ego on the shelf and take a good hard look at the wreckage of your past. If you truly desire to serve others, it's time to get humble and start making that list.

Is making amends always necessary for successful recovery, or are there exceptions?

In successful recovery, making amends is often necessary for peace of mind and repairing relationships. Although there may be exceptions, being willing to make things right with those we've harmed can bring a sense of closure and personal growth.

Conclusion

As we conclude our journey through Step Eight, we take a deep breath and reflect on all that's transpired. We've faced our demons head-on, confronted the wreckage of our past, and taken responsibility for the harm we've caused others.

Like a phoenix rising from the ashes, we're reborn with a newfound sense of purpose and commitment to change. Through this process, we've gained a deeper understanding of ourselves and those around us. We've learned to examine our actions and their impact on others with clear eyes and an open heart.

As we move forward towards making amends, we know that challenges will arise. But with the support and guidance of our fellow members, we'll overcome them. In this moment of healing and recovery, we celebrate not just individual growth but collective transformation towards a better tomorrow.

STEP NINE

We Made Direct Amends to Such People Wherever Possible, Except When to Do So Would Injure Them or Others

We've all made mistakes in our lives, whether big or small. Some of these mistakes may have hurt the people we care about, and we may feel guilty or ashamed as a result. But what can we do to make things right? How can we repair the damage that has been done and move forward in a positive direction?

Well, it just so happens that Step Nine of the recovery process has some answers for us. This step involves making direct amends to the people we have harmed, wherever possible. It's not always easy to face up to our mistakes and take responsibility for our actions, but this step is an important part of the healing process.

So let's dive into Step Nine and explore how we can make meaningful amends and repair damaged relationships with others.

Understanding the Importance of Step Nine in the Recovery Process

You're probably feeling nervous about facing the people you've wronged, but taking this step and making amends is crucial for your recovery and will help you find peace in your relationships. Step Nine is an important part of the recovery process because it allows us to take responsibility for our actions and repair the damage we have caused. It's not easy to confront those we have hurt, but it's necessary if we want to move forward with our lives.

Making direct amends means taking action to make things right with those we have harmed. This can include apologizing, paying back debts, or doing whatever else is necessary to address the harm that has been done. It's important to do this wherever possible, but there may be situations where making amends would cause more harm than good. In these cases, it's important to consider the potential consequences before making a decision.

When we make direct amends, we show that we are committed to changing our behavior and repairing our relationships. We acknowledge the pain that we have caused others and take steps to make things right. This can be a powerful experience both for ourselves and for those we are making amends with. By taking responsibility for our actions and showing genuine remorse, we give ourselves and others the opportunity to heal.

Step Nine is a crucial part of the recovery process because it allows us to take responsibility for our actions and repair the damage that has been done. While it can be difficult and uncomfortable at times, making direct amends is necessary if we want to move forward in our lives with integrity and peace of mind.

By approaching this step with an open heart and a willingness to serve others, we can begin building stronger connections with those around us while also strengthening our own recovery journey.

Identifying the People We Need to Make Amends To

Identifying the individuals that require our amends is a crucial step in this process, and it's important to approach this with honesty and sincerity. We need to take an honest inventory of our past actions and behaviors that may have caused harm or hurt to others. This requires self-reflection and taking responsibility for our actions without blaming others.

It's important to note that making amends isn't always easy, but it's necessary for both parties involved. We should make every effort possible to reach out directly to those we've harmed and offer a sincere apology. It can be helpful to prepare what we want to say beforehand so that we express ourselves clearly and honestly.

Sometimes, however, making direct amends isn't possible or appropriate. In these situations, we need to find alternative ways of making things right or showing remorse. For example, if the individual has passed away or is no longer in our lives, we can make a donation in their honor or perform a kind act for someone else as a way of acknowledging the harm we caused.

Ultimately, identifying who we need to make amends with takes courage and humility. It may not be easy at first, but by taking responsibility for our past actions and doing what we can to make things right, we are on the path towards healing ourselves and rebuilding relationships with those around us.

Preparing for the Amends Process

Before diving into the amends process, it's important for us to take a step back and reflect on our past actions and behaviors. We need to approach this step with sincerity, empathy, and a willingness to make things right. It can be difficult to admit our wrongdoings and face the people we have hurt, but it is necessary for our own growth and healing.

Preparing for the amends process involves more than just identifying the people we need to make amends to. We need to take time to consider what we'll say and how we'll say it. It's important that we're honest about what happened without making excuses or placing blame on others.

We also need to be prepared for different reactions from the people we're making amends to - they may not be ready or willing to forgive us right away.

It can be helpful to seek guidance from a sponsor or trusted friend before making amends. They can offer support and help us work through any fears or doubts we may have about this process. Additionally, practicing self-care during this time is crucial as it can bring up intense emotions that may be difficult to navigate alone.

Preparing for the amends process requires reflection, honesty, and support from others. It's important that we approach this step with sincerity and empathy towards those who have been hurt by our actions. By doing so, we can begin repairing damaged relationships and ultimately find peace within ourselves.

Making Amends in a Meaningful and Respectful Way

Making amends can be a difficult process, but it's well worth the effort. Studies have shown that 80% of people who made amends reported feeling happier and more at peace with themselves. This is because making amends lifts a heavy burden off our shoulders and gives us a chance to repair relationships that may have been damaged in the past.

To make amends in a meaningful and respectful way, it's important to remember that this process isn't about seeking forgiveness or absolution from others. It's about taking responsibility for our own actions and showing genuine remorse for any harm we may have caused.

Here are three ways to do so:

1. Be specific: When making amends, it's important to be specific about what you're apologizing for and how you plan to make things right. This shows that you've taken the time to reflect on your actions and are committed to making things right.
2. Listen actively: In some cases, the person you're making amends with may want to express their own hurt or frustration over what happened. It's important to listen actively without interrupting or getting defensive - this shows that you respect their feelings and are willing to hear them out.
3. Follow through: Making amends isn't just about saying sorry - it also involves taking action to make things right. Whether it's paying back money owed or following through on promises made, it's important to show that you're committed to changing your behavior moving forward.

Making amends can be a challenging but ultimately rewarding process. By being specific, listening actively, and following through on our commitments, we can show genuine remorse for our actions and work towards repairing any damage caused by our past mistakes.

As we take these steps towards healing broken relationships, we also cultivate a deeper sense of empathy and compassion towards others - something that ultimately benefits both ourselves and those around us.

Taking Responsibility for Our Actions

Taking responsibility for our actions is crucial in personal growth and development, as it allows us to learn from our mistakes and make positive changes moving forward. In step nine of the twelve-step program, we take this responsibility one step further by making direct amends to those we have harmed.

This process can be challenging but also incredibly rewarding. Making amends requires humility and vulnerability, as we must face the consequences of our actions and seek forgiveness from those we have wronged. It is important to approach these conversations with sincerity and a willingness to listen to the other person's perspective. By doing so, we can begin to repair damaged relationships and move towards healing.

However, it is also important to recognize that not all situations are appropriate for direct amends. If reaching out would cause harm or further pain for the other person or others involved, it may be best to refrain from doing so. In these cases, we must find alternative ways to make things right and continue working towards making positive changes in our lives.

Ultimately, taking responsibility for our actions through direct amends allows us to break free from the cycle of guilt and shame that often accompanies addiction. By showing accountability for past mistakes and actively working towards making things right, we can move forward with a newfound sense of purpose and self-awareness.

Acknowledging the Hurt We Have Caused Others

Acknowledging the hurt we've caused others can be a painful but necessary step towards healing and rebuilding damaged relationships.

In Step Nine of our recovery journey, we make direct amends to those whom we have wronged. It's important that we do this wherever possible, except when doing so would cause further harm.

Making amends is not about seeking forgiveness or absolution from others. Rather, it's about taking responsibility for our actions and acknowledging the impact they have had on those around us.

We must be willing to listen to their experiences and validate the pain they have endured as a result of our behavior. This process requires humility, honesty, and vulnerability on our part.

We must be willing to admit when we are wrong and take action to make things right. This may involve making financial reparations or offering a sincere apology, but it always involves showing up with an open heart and a willingness to listen.

Ultimately, making amends is about repairing relationships that have been damaged by our behavior. It's an opportunity for us to show others that we value them and their feelings above our own ego or pride.

By doing so, we can begin to rebuild trust and create a foundation for healthier interactions in the future.

Seeking Forgiveness and Repairing Relationships

Now that we've acknowledged the hurt we've caused others, it's time to take action towards repairing those relationships. Step Nine of the Twelve Steps outlines this process and encourages us to make direct amends to those we've wronged, whenever possible.

Making amends means taking responsibility for our actions and seeking forgiveness from those we've harmed. It also involves making reparations or restitution in whatever way is appropriate. This can be a difficult and humbling process, but it's an essential step towards healing both ourselves and our relationships with others.

It's important to note that there may be situations where making direct amends would actually cause more harm than good. In these cases, it's crucial to seek guidance from a sponsor or other trusted advisor in navigating the situation. Ultimately, our goal should always be to act in a way that serves both ourselves and others.

By making direct amends wherever possible, we demonstrate our commitment to living a life of integrity and service. We acknowledge the pain we've caused others, take responsibility for our actions, and work towards repairing any damage done.

Through this process of seeking forgiveness and making amends, we can begin to rebuild trust with those around us and move forward on a path of healing and growth.

Dealing with Resistance or Rejection

Don't be surprised if some people resist or reject your attempts to make amends - after all, you did cause them pain and hurt. It takes courage to face those whom we have wronged and ask for forgiveness. But even with the best intentions, not everyone will be receptive to our apologies.

Some may still be angry or hurt, or simply choose not to forgive us. When faced with resistance or rejection, it's important to remember that we cannot control other people's reactions. We can only control our own actions and behavior.

If someone does not want to accept our apology, we must respect their wishes and give them space. It may take time for wounds to heal, and in some cases it may never happen.

It's also important to consider whether making amends would further harm the person or others involved. In these situations, we must weigh the potential consequences of our actions before proceeding. Sometimes the best course of action is simply letting go and moving on, while still taking responsibility for our past mistakes.

Ultimately, making direct amends is about taking responsibility for our past mistakes and doing what we can to repair relationships that have been damaged by our actions. While it may not always be easy or successful in every case, it's a crucial step in our journey toward recovery and becoming better versions of ourselves.

By keeping an open mind and heart, we can continue learning from our mistakes and striving towards a brighter future.

Maintaining Accountability and Continuing the Healing Process

Maintaining accountability and continuing the healing process requires constant effort and a willingness to reflect on our actions. As we work through step nine, it's important to remember that making amends isn't just about apologizing for past mistakes - it's about taking responsibility for our actions and actively working to repair the harm we've caused.

One way to stay accountable during this process is by regularly checking in with a sponsor or trusted friend. By sharing our progress with someone we trust, we can gain valuable insight into how our actions are impacting those around us. This can help us identify areas where we need to make further amends or change our behavior moving forward.

It's also important to be patient and compassionate with ourselves as we navigate this step. Making amends can be a difficult and emotional process, especially when dealing with past traumas or hurtful behaviors. But by staying committed to the healing process, we can begin to repair relationships and build healthier connections with others.

Ultimately, continuing the work of step nine means recognizing that making amends is an ongoing journey rather than a one-time event. We may encounter resistance or setbacks along the way, but by staying focused on accountability and growth, we can continue to heal ourselves and serve those around us in meaningful ways.

Celebrating Progress and Moving Forward in Recovery

As you celebrate your progress and move forward in recovery, it's important to acknowledge the hard work you've put in and the positive changes you've made.

For example, one person may have struggled with addiction for years but now has several months of sobriety under their belt, allowing them to rebuild relationships and pursue new passions.

Reflecting on your journey can be a powerful way to recognize how far you've come. Take some time to write down all of the positive changes that have happened since starting recovery. This could include things like repairing damaged relationships, finding new hobbies or interests, or simply feeling more at peace with yourself.

It's also important to remember that recovery is an ongoing process. While celebrating progress is important, it's equally crucial to keep moving forward and continuing to work on personal growth and healing. This might mean seeking out additional support from a therapist or support group, or simply taking time each day for self-reflection and self-care.

Ultimately, as we continue on our path towards healing and serving others, it's vital that we stay committed to making amends wherever possible. Whether this means apologizing for past mistakes or being there for someone who needs us now, true recovery involves taking responsibility for our actions and doing what we can to make things right.

So let's continue on this journey together - celebrating progress while staying focused on growth and helping those around us whenever possible.

Frequently Asked Questions

What are some common reasons why someone may resist making amends?

Making amends can be difficult due to fear, shame, or pride. We may worry about rejection or hurting others. However, it's important to remember that healing relationships is a powerful act of service both for ourselves and those we have harmed.

Can making amends ever be harmful to the person we are apologizing to or others involved?

Making amends can have potential harm but is necessary for our own growth and healing. We must approach with humility, empathy, and respect. It's crucial to consider the other person's feelings and well-being before making amends.

How can we determine if making amends is truly necessary and beneficial for all parties involved?

We determine the necessity of making amends by examining our motives and consequences. We seek to benefit all parties involved, not just ourselves. As we serve others with humility, clarity arises for right action.

What are some strategies for repairing relationships that have been severely damaged by our actions?

When repairing damaged relationships, we must act like a gardener, patiently tending to each plant's unique needs. We listen, offer sincere apologies and make amends in ways that are meaningful to the other person.

How can we maintain accountability and continue the healing process after making amends?

After making amends, we continue to take responsibility for our actions and prioritize the needs of those we have harmed. We actively listen, practice empathy, and make changes to prevent future harm. Our goal is to rebuild trust and show we are committed to their well-being.

Conclusion

In the end, step nine is all about repairing the broken relationships that we've caused through our addiction. It's not an easy process, but it's necessary if we want to truly heal and move forward in recovery.

Through direct amends, we take responsibility for our actions and seek forgiveness from those we've hurt along the way. As we complete this step, it's important to remember that healing takes time.

We may face resistance or rejection from those we're making amends to, but staying accountable and continuing to work on ourselves can help us stay on track. And as difficult as it may be, celebrating our progress along the way can give us the motivation to keep moving forward towards a brighter future free from addiction.

STEP TEN

We Continued To Take Personal Inventory and When
We Were Wrong Promptly Admitted It

I know what you might be thinking - 'Another story about addiction recovery? Haven't we read enough already?'

But hear me out. Recovery from addiction is not a one-and-done process. It's an ongoing journey, filled with ups and downs, victories and setbacks.

And Step Ten - 'We continued to take personal inventory and when we were wrong promptly admitted it'- is a crucial part of that journey.

In Step Ten, we learn the importance of regularly reflecting on our thoughts, feelings, and actions. We recognize patterns of harmful behavior and work to avoid relapse through self-awareness.

By developing honesty, humility, and self-awareness through ongoing personal inventory and admission of wrongdoing, we can achieve long-term sobriety.

So let's dive deeper into what Step Ten entails and how it fits into the overall recovery process.

The Importance of Ongoing Recovery in Addiction

Keep up the good work by continuing to take personal inventory and promptly admitting when you're wrong - it's an essential part of ongoing recovery in addiction!

This step is critical because it helps us stay grounded and aware of our actions, thoughts, and emotions. We can learn a lot about ourselves through taking regular inventory, which can help us identify triggers and patterns that may lead to relapse.

Continuing to take personal inventory also means being accountable for our actions. It takes courage to admit when we're wrong or have made mistakes, but doing so is crucial for maintaining healthy relationships with ourselves and others.

When we ignore our shortcomings or deflect blame onto others, we ultimately hurt ourselves and those around us. Admitting mistakes promptly can be challenging at times, especially if we feel ashamed or embarrassed. However, acknowledging our errors allows us to grow and improve as individuals.

It also shows integrity and respect towards those affected by our actions. By taking responsibility for our mistakes, we demonstrate a willingness to make amends and learn from past experiences.

The tenth step emphasizes the importance of self-reflection and accountability in ongoing recovery from addiction. It encourages us to continue taking personal inventory regularly while admitting any wrongdoing promptly.

By doing so, we gain insight into ourselves while building stronger connections with loved ones through honesty and vulnerability. Remember that recovery is a journey that requires commitment to growth – keep up the good work!

How Step Ten Fits into the Recovery Process

Maintaining a thorough self-awareness regimen is an integral component of successful recovery, ensuring that individuals remain accountable and responsible for their actions. This is where step ten comes in, as it focuses on the ongoing process of taking personal inventory and admitting when we're wrong promptly. In other words, it's about staying honest with ourselves and others as we continue on our path to sobriety.

Step ten encourages us to reflect daily on our thoughts, feelings, and actions. By doing so, we can identify any negative patterns or behaviors that may be hindering our progress. It's important to remember that recovery doesn't end after completing the 12 steps; it's a lifelong journey that requires constant effort and diligence.

Through regular self-reflection, we can develop greater insight into who we are as individuals and learn more about our triggers or vulnerabilities. This knowledge allows us to make better decisions in the future and avoid relapse. Admitting when we're wrong also helps us maintain healthy relationships with those around us by promoting open communication and transparency.

Step ten plays a vital role in the recovery process by encouraging ongoing self-analysis and accountability. By remaining mindful of our thoughts, feelings, and actions, we can continue to grow both personally and spiritually while maintaining sobriety. It requires effort but through dedication and commitment - success is possible!

Defining Personal Inventory in Step Ten

When you regularly reflect on your thoughts, feelings, and actions through Step Ten, it's like taking a daily snapshot of yourself to identify any negative patterns or behaviors that may be hindering your progress.

Personal inventory is the process of self-reflection that allows us to assess our behavior and emotions in order to understand how we can improve ourselves. By continuing to take personal inventory, we are able to stay accountable for our actions and address any character defects that may come up.

Here are three ways in which taking personal inventory can benefit us:

- It helps us stay mindful: When we make a habit of reflecting on our thoughts and actions throughout the day, we become more mindful of how we're showing up in the world. This increased awareness allows us to catch negative patterns before they become habits.
- It promotes honest communication: Being truthful with ourselves about our shortcomings allows us to be more authentic with others. We're better equipped to admit when we're wrong and apologize promptly when necessary.
- It fosters growth: Taking personal inventory provides an opportunity for growth by allowing us to identify areas where we need improvement. Through continued self-reflection, we can work towards becoming the best versions of ourselves.

Promptly admitting when we're wrong is an essential part of Step Ten. It requires humility and courage, but ultimately leads to deeper connections with those around us as well as greater self-awareness. As a result, taking personal inventory becomes less daunting over time as it becomes second nature in our daily lives.

The Benefits of Reflecting on Thoughts, Feelings, and Actions

Mindfully monitoring our thoughts, feelings, and actions can enhance our honesty, humility, and personal growth. When we take personal inventory regularly, we become more aware of our behavior patterns and how they may affect those around us. We start to see the areas where we need improvement and can take steps towards making meaningful changes.

Reflecting on our thoughts allows us to identify negative thought patterns that may be holding us back from reaching our full potential. We can challenge these thoughts by replacing them with positive affirmations that align with our goals. By acknowledging and addressing negative self-talk, we can improve our self-esteem and confidence.

When we reflect on our feelings, we gain a deeper understanding of ourselves and others. We learn to recognize triggers that may cause strong emotions such as anger or anxiety. This awareness allows us to respond in a more constructive way rather than reacting impulsively. As a result, we build stronger relationships based on empathy and compassion.

Taking inventory of our actions helps us stay accountable for the choices we make. It allows us to recognize when we have acted in a way that doesn't align with our values or hurts others. Promptly admitting when we're wrong shows integrity and builds trust with those around us.

When we consistently practice taking personal inventory, it becomes easier to acknowledge mistakes without fear of judgment or shame. Reflecting on thoughts, feelings, and actions is an essential part of personal growth. By being mindful of ourselves in this way, not only do we benefit from becoming better versions of ourselves but also serve others better by creating healthier relationships built upon mutual respect and understanding.

Recognizing Patterns of Harmful Behavior

Recognizing patterns of harmful behavior can be challenging, but it's an important step towards personal growth and building healthier relationships. It requires a willingness to take a hard look at ourselves and acknowledge the ways in which we may have hurt others. This kind of self-reflection can be uncomfortable, but it's necessary if we want to become better people.

One way to recognize patterns of harmful behavior is by examining our past actions and interactions with others. We can ask ourselves questions like: Have I consistently treated others with kindness and respect? Have I been honest in my dealings with others, or have I lied or manipulated them? Have I shown empathy towards those who are different from me, or have I been judgmental or intolerant?

Another way to identify patterns of harmful behavior is by paying attention to our thoughts and feelings. Do we find ourselves feeling angry or resentful towards certain people or situations? Do we tend to blame others for our problems instead of taking responsibility for our own actions? Do we struggle with feelings of jealousy or envy towards those who seem more successful than us?

Recognizing patterns of harmful behavior involves being willing to admit when we're wrong and take steps to make amends. This means apologizing sincerely when we've hurt someone else, committing to changing our behavior moving forward, and seeking help if necessary. By taking these steps, we not only improve our relationships with others but also grow as individuals.

In conclusion, recognizing patterns of harmful behavior is essential for personal growth and building healthy relationships. It requires honesty, self-reflection, and a willingness to take responsibility for our actions. By examining our past behaviors and current thoughts and feelings, we can identify areas where we need improvement and take steps towards becoming better people. Ultimately, this process benefits not only ourselves but also those around us as we strive towards serving others in all aspects of life.

Taking Responsibility for Mistakes

As we continue on the path of recovery, it's important to recognize patterns of harmful behavior and take responsibility for our mistakes. This involves being honest with ourselves about our shortcomings and actively working to make amends for any harm we've caused.

Taking personal inventory is a crucial step in this process. It allows us to reflect on our actions, thoughts, and feelings, and identify areas where we may have fallen short. By doing so, we can make a conscious effort to correct these behaviors and prevent them from causing further harm.

However, it's not enough to simply acknowledge our mistakes - we must also be willing to admit them promptly. This means taking ownership of our actions and apologizing if necessary. It can be difficult to admit when we're wrong, but doing so is an essential part of growth and healing.

Ultimately, taking personal inventory and admitting when we're wrong helps us become better versions of ourselves. By acknowledging our flaws and working to correct them, we become more compassionate, empathetic individuals who are better equipped to serve others in meaningful ways.

Avoiding Relapse through Self-Awareness

Avoiding relapse requires being self-aware of our triggers and making conscious efforts to address them in order to maintain sobriety. It's not enough to simply acknowledge that we've made mistakes in the past.

We need to actively work towards preventing those same mistakes from happening again. Taking personal inventory means taking a look at ourselves, our actions, and our motivations on a regular basis. By doing this, we can identify potential triggers that may lead us back down the path of addiction.

This level of self-awareness allows us to take proactive steps towards avoiding these triggers before they become an issue. When we do make mistakes or find ourselves falling into old patterns, it's important to promptly admit it.

This isn't always easy - admitting fault can be difficult for anyone - but it's necessary if we want to avoid slipping back into old habits. By owning up to our wrongs, we can begin the process of correcting them and moving forward with a clear mind and conscience.

By continuing this process of personal inventory and prompt admission of faults as outlined in step ten, we're better equipped to face life's challenges without relying on addictive behaviors as a coping mechanism. Ultimately, this leads to greater fulfillment not only for ourselves but also for those around us as we become more capable of serving others with integrity and honesty.

Developing Honesty, Humility, and Self-Awareness

Developing honesty, humility, and self-awareness is crucial in maintaining sobriety and living a fulfilling life free from addictive behaviors. This step involves taking personal inventory of our thoughts, actions, and attitudes on a regular basis.

We must be willing to admit when we're wrong promptly and make amends if necessary. Without these essential qualities, it becomes difficult to maintain healthy relationships with ourselves and others.

Self-awareness is an integral part of this process because it allows us to recognize patterns of behavior that may lead us down the path of addiction once again. By identifying our triggers and learning how to cope with them effectively, we can avoid relapse altogether.

Honesty comes into play when we acknowledge our shortcomings without judgment or shame. Humility allows us to admit that we don't have all the answers and need help from others at times.

This step is not just about admitting when we're wrong; it's also about acknowledging our strengths and accomplishments along the way. Celebrating small victories helps build self-esteem and gives us the motivation to keep going.

When we take personal inventory regularly, it becomes easier to see progress over time. Developing honesty, humility, and self-awareness is essential for anyone seeking long-term recovery from addiction. It requires a willingness to look within ourselves honestly and without judgment while recognizing that change takes time.

By embracing these qualities as a way of life rather than just a one-time practice, we can achieve lasting happiness in sobriety while serving as an example for those around us who may be struggling with similar issues.

Applying Step Ten in Daily Life

By regularly practicing Step Ten, we can keep our sobriety on course like a skilled sailor navigating through rough waters. This step involves taking personal inventory and admitting promptly when we're wrong. It may seem daunting at first, but with time it becomes second nature.

Here are some ways to apply Step Ten in our daily lives:

- Take a moment each day to reflect on how we've treated others and ourselves.
- Ask ourselves if there's anything we need to make amends for or apologize for.
- Be aware of any negative emotions that arise and work to address them before they escalate.
- When we do make mistakes, take responsibility and make amends as soon as possible.
- Celebrate our progress by acknowledging the positive changes in our behavior.

When we practice Step Ten consistently, it helps us stay accountable and avoid falling back into old patterns of behavior. We become more self-aware and learn to recognize when our thoughts or actions might be harmful to ourselves or others. By taking responsibility for our mistakes and making amends promptly, we demonstrate humility and show that we value the relationships in our lives.

Applying this step also helps us cultivate gratitude for the progress we've made so far. We can acknowledge that recovery is an ongoing journey, but by staying committed to self-reflection and growth, we continue to move forward towards a healthier life. Ultimately, practicing Step Ten allows us to live with integrity and authenticity while also serving those around us by being honest about who we are and what motivates us.

Long-Term Sobriety Through Ongoing Personal Inventory and Admission of Wrongdoing

Maintaining long-term sobriety requires regularly practicing personal inventory and admitting wrongdoing. It's not enough to just go through the 12 steps once and think that our work is done. We must continue to look within ourselves on a daily basis, taking stock of our thoughts, actions, and behaviors. By doing so, we can catch any negative patterns before they become destructive.

This ongoing process of personal inventory also helps us stay connected with our higher power. When we take a thorough and honest look at ourselves, we're better able to see where we may have strayed from the path of recovery and where we need help to get back on track. Admitting when we're wrong allows us to be humble and open-minded, which are essential traits for maintaining sobriety.

By regularly practicing step ten, we also improve our relationships with others. When we admit our mistakes promptly, it shows respect for others and their feelings. It also allows us to make amends quickly if necessary, before any damage is done. This level of accountability fosters trust and deeper connections with those around us.

Ultimately, step ten helps us live a more fulfilled life by keeping us mindful of our actions and how they impact those around us. It allows us to grow as individuals while staying true to the principles of recovery. By continuing this practice even after achieving long-term sobriety, we can ensure that our journey towards self-improvement never ends.

Frequently Asked Questions

What are the other steps in the recovery process besides Step Ten?

In addition to Step Ten, there are twelve steps in the recovery process. These steps involve admitting powerlessness over addiction, seeking guidance from a higher power, making amends for wrongs done, and helping others struggling with addiction.

Can Step Ten be skipped or avoided in the recovery process?

Skipping Step Ten in our recovery process can hinder our growth and lead to relapse. Admitting our wrongs helps us maintain humility and improve relationships. It's important to stay accountable for our actions.

How can individuals improve their self-awareness and ability to recognize harmful behavior patterns?

To improve our self-awareness and recognize harmful behavior patterns, we must actively seek feedback from others and reflect on our actions. We can also practice mindfulness techniques to become more present in the moment and better understand our thoughts and emotions.

Are there any potential drawbacks or challenges to regularly taking personal inventory?

Regularly taking personal inventory can be challenging as it requires humility and vulnerability. It may also bring up uncomfortable emotions and force us to confront our mistakes. However, the benefits of growth and self-improvement outweigh any potential drawbacks.

How does admitting wrongdoing and making amends contribute to long-term sobriety?

Admitting our wrongdoings and making amends allows us to take responsibility for our actions and repair damaged relationships. This fosters a sense of accountability, humility, and compassion, which are essential for long-term sobriety and serving others.

Conclusion

So there you have it, step ten of our recovery process - continuing to take personal inventory and admitting when we're wrong.

It may seem like a daunting task, but the benefits are immeasurable. By reflecting on our thoughts, feelings, and actions, we can recognize patterns of harmful behavior and avoid relapse through self-awareness.

Studies show that those who regularly practice step ten have a higher likelihood of long-term sobriety than those who don't. Imagine being able to look back after years of sobriety and knowing that your commitment to ongoing personal inventory and admission of wrongdoing played a crucial role in your success.

It's all possible with Step Ten - so why not give it a try? The rewards are certainly worth it.

STEP ELEVEN

We Sought Through Prayer and Meditation to Improve Our Conscious Contact with God As We Understood Him, Praying Only For Knowledge of His Will for Us and the Power to Carry That Out

Step Eleven is where the magic happens. It's like opening a door to a world beyond our own, one that we can only access through prayer and meditation. This step is the gateway to improving our conscious contact with God as we understand Him, and it's an essential part of our recovery journey.

As I reflect on my experience with Step Eleven, I can't help but feel grateful for the power of prayer and meditation in my life. It's like having a direct line to a higher power, one that provides me with guidance and strength when I need it most.

And while this step may seem daunting at first, it's actually quite simple once you understand its meaning and purpose. So let's dive into Step Eleven together and explore how it can improve our lives in ways we never thought possible.

The Importance of a Higher Power in Recovery

You'll be amazed at how important a higher power can be in your recovery. When we first enter recovery, we often feel lost and alone. Addiction has taken over our lives, and we don't know where to turn. That's where a higher power comes in.

By believing in something greater than ourselves, whether it's God, the universe, or simply the idea of goodness, we open ourselves up to new possibilities. Sought through prayer and meditation to improve our conscious contact with God as we understood him is an important step in this process. Through these practices, we can connect more deeply with our higher power and gain clarity about what their will may be for us.

It's not about asking for things or trying to control outcomes; it's about surrendering to something greater than ourselves and trusting that things will work out as they should. Praying only for knowledge of his will for us and the power to carry that out is another crucial aspect of this step. We're not asking for specific outcomes or material possessions; instead, we're seeking guidance on how best to live our lives in accordance with our values and beliefs.

By letting go of our own desires and focusing on what's truly important, we can find a sense of peace and purpose that was missing before. Seeking through prayer and meditation to improve our conscious contact with God as we understand him is vital to successful recovery. It helps us connect with something greater than ourselves, gain clarity about what's truly important, and let go of our own desires so that we can live according to a higher purpose.

If you haven't already incorporated this practice into your recovery program, I encourage you to give it a try – the results may surprise you!

Understanding the Meaning of Step Eleven

To fully embrace the program, don't you need to understand how Step Eleven can help you improve your relationship with a higher power and gain the strength to follow His plan? This step is all about seeking through prayer and meditation to improve our conscious contact with God as we understand Him. But what does that really mean? Let's break it down into three sub-lists:

- What is conscious contact? Conscious contact means being aware of and connected to our higher power throughout our daily lives. It means actively seeking guidance, comfort, and strength from God in every moment.
- How can prayer and meditation help us achieve conscious contact? Prayer is a way for us to communicate with God and express our gratitude, fears, hopes, and needs. Meditation allows us to quiet our minds so we can listen for God's guidance and messages. Together, these practices enable us to build a deeper relationship with God.
- Why do we pray only for knowledge of His will for us? This part of the step reminds us that we are not in control of everything; there is a higher power at work in our lives. By praying only for knowledge of His will for us (not selfish desires or outcomes), we become more willing to let go of our own agendas and trust that God's plan is better than ours.

As we deepen our conscious contact with God through prayer and meditation, we begin to experience amazing changes in ourselves: increased serenity, clarity of mind, compassion for others, willingness to serve others. We begin to see life from a new perspective – one where we are no longer alone but part of something much greater than ourselves. We also gain the power necessary to carry out His will because when we align ourselves with God's purpose for our lives, anything becomes possible.

Step Eleven invites us to explore spirituality beyond mere religious rituals or beliefs by showing us how prayer and meditation can bring profound transformation into every aspect of our lives. It teaches us to rely on a higher power for guidance and strength, to trust in His plan, and to serve others selflessly. By practicing this step regularly, we can experience an unshakable sense of peace and purpose that will sustain us through the ups and downs of life.

The Role of Prayer in Step Eleven

When you open your heart to prayer, you invite a powerful force into your life that can transform everything.

In Step Eleven, we seek to improve our conscious contact with God through prayer and meditation. But what's the role of prayer in this step? Prayer serves as a way for us to communicate with God and express our desires and needs. It helps us connect with a higher power that can guide us towards fulfilling our purpose.

Prayer also plays an important role in Step Eleven by helping us align our will with God's will for us. As we pray only for knowledge of His will and the power to carry it out, we let go of our own desires and trust in God's plan for our lives. Through prayer, we become more receptive to the guidance and wisdom that comes from a divine source rather than relying solely on our own understanding.

Furthermore, prayer helps build a stronger relationship between ourselves and God. By taking time each day to pray and meditate, we deepen our connection with the divine. This connection allows us to experience peace, comfort, and guidance even during times of difficulty or uncertainty.

Prayer is an essential aspect of Step Eleven as it helps improve our conscious contact with God while allowing us to align ourselves with His will for us. It provides a means for communication between ourselves and a higher power while building a deeper relationship with Him. When we open ourselves up to the power of prayer, we invite transformation into every area of our lives.

The Role of Meditation in Step Eleven

By quieting our minds and focusing on our breath, we can tap into a deeper sense of spirituality during Step Eleven. Meditation allows us to clear our minds of distractions and connect with a higher power. It helps us develop a greater awareness of ourselves and the world around us, leading to renewed energy and fresh perspectives on life's challenges.

To make the most out of meditation, it's important to set aside time each day for this practice. Find a quiet space where you won't be disturbed, sit comfortably with your back straight, close your eyes, and focus on your breath. As thoughts arise (which they inevitably will), gently acknowledge them without judgment or attachment, then return your attention to your breath. Over time, this practice will become easier and more natural.

Incorporating gratitude into our meditation practice is another powerful way to deepen our spiritual connection during Step Eleven. Reflecting on all that we have to be grateful for in life can help shift our perspective from one of lack or struggle to one of abundance and possibility. By regularly expressing thanks for even the smallest blessings in life, we cultivate a positive mindset that can help us stay centered in times of difficulty.

Remember that there are many different forms of meditation – from guided meditations led by an instructor to simple mindfulness practices that you can do anywhere at any time. The key is finding what works best for you personally and making it a regular part of your daily routine.

With consistent effort over time, meditation can become an invaluable tool for improving our conscious contact with God as we understand Him during Step Eleven. It can help us gain clarity about His will for us and find the strength we need to carry it out every day.

How to Establish Conscious Contact with a Higher Power

Establishing conscious contact with a higher power can be achieved through daily spiritual practices such as meditation, prayer, and gratitude. These practices allow us to quiet our minds and connect with a power greater than ourselves.

Through prayer, we can ask for guidance and understanding of our higher power's will for us. We can also express gratitude for the blessings in our lives, which reinforces our connection with this higher power.

Meditation is another powerful tool that helps us improve our conscious contact with a higher power. By focusing on our breath or repeating a mantra, we can quiet the chatter in our minds and become more receptive to guidance from the universe. Regular meditation practice cultivates inner peace and clarity of mind, which enables us to better discern between ego-driven desires and the voice of our higher power.

In addition to these spiritual practices, it's important to cultivate an attitude of willingness and openness towards serving others. When we focus on giving rather than receiving, we align ourselves with the energy of the universe and become more attuned to its workings. This selflessness allows us to receive guidance from a place beyond ourselves.

Ultimately, establishing conscious contact with a higher power requires consistent effort over time. It's not something that happens overnight but rather through diligent practice day after day. By making spirituality a priority in our lives, we open ourselves up to living in harmony with something greater than ourselves – an experience that brings profound meaning and purpose into every aspect of life.

Defining Your Higher Power

Now that we've learned how to establish conscious contact with our higher power, let's dive deeper into defining who or what that higher power may be.

For some, it may be a traditional religious deity, while for others it could be the universe or nature itself. It's important to understand that there's no right or wrong answer when it comes to defining your higher power – what matters most is that you find something that resonates with you and helps guide you towards living a fulfilling life.

One way to define your higher power is by reflecting on experiences where you felt a strong sense of connection or guidance from something greater than yourself. This could be through prayer, meditation, nature walks, or any other spiritual practice.

By identifying these moments and analyzing what made them powerful for you personally, you can start to gain a better understanding of what your higher power means to you.

Another approach is to consider the values and principles that are most important in your life. Your higher power may embody qualities such as love, compassion, forgiveness, or strength – whatever traits align with your personal beliefs and goals.

By focusing on these attributes and incorporating them into your daily thoughts and actions, you can strengthen your connection with your higher power and live in alignment with its will for you.

Ultimately, the goal of step eleven isn't necessarily about finding the perfect definition of a higher power – rather, it's about cultivating an ongoing relationship with something bigger than ourselves. By seeking out opportunities for prayer and meditation and asking only for knowledge of our higher power's will for us (rather than making demands), we open ourselves up to receiving guidance and support along our journey towards recovery and personal growth.

Asking for Guidance and Strength in Recovery

How can we ask for guidance and strength in our recovery without making demands on our higher power? The answer lies in the eleventh step of the twelve-step program.

By seeking through prayer and meditation to improve our conscious contact with God as we understand him, we open ourselves up to receiving knowledge of his will for us and the power to carry that out. This means that instead of asking for specific outcomes or solutions, we ask for the wisdom and courage to do what's right.

Asking for guidance and strength in this way requires humility and surrender. We must acknowledge that we can't control everything, including our addiction or compulsive behavior. By admitting our powerlessness, we make space for a higher power to work in our lives. This doesn't mean that we give up responsibility or agency; rather, it means that we recognize the limits of our own abilities and seek support from a source beyond ourselves.

Prayer and meditation are powerful tools for cultivating a relationship with a higher power. Through these practices, we can quiet our minds, connect with something greater than ourselves, and listen deeply for guidance. It's important to remember that there's no one 'right' way to pray or meditate - what matters most is sincerity and regularity.

In recovery, asking for guidance and strength from a higher power isn't just about getting what we want; it's about aligning ourselves with a greater purpose. As members of a community dedicated to serving others, we must be willing to set aside personal desires in order to fulfill our obligations to each other and the world at large.

When we pray only for knowledge of God's will for us and the power to carry it out, we become vessels through which love can flow freely into the world.

The Benefits of Step Eleven in Daily Life

By regularly practicing prayer and meditation to improve our connection with a higher power, we can experience numerous benefits in daily life. While step eleven is an integral part of the recovery process, it also has significant implications for our overall well-being.

As we seek to understand God's will for us, we learn to let go of our own desires and trust in a higher power. This sense of surrender allows us to find peace amidst life's many challenges.

Through prayer and meditation, we develop greater awareness of ourselves and our surroundings. We become more attuned to the needs of others and are better equipped to serve those around us. This heightened sense of empathy helps us build stronger relationships, both within our families and communities. By focusing on what truly matters - love, compassion, and understanding - we create a positive ripple effect that can transform entire communities.

Step eleven also teaches us the importance of self-reflection. In today's fast-paced world, it's all too easy to lose sight of what really matters in life. By taking time each day to reflect on our actions, thoughts, and feelings, we gain greater insight into how they impact ourselves and others. This newfound clarity enables us to make better decisions moving forward.

Ultimately, step eleven is about cultivating a deep sense of spiritual connection with the world around us. By doing so, we unlock countless opportunities for growth and fulfillment in all areas of life - from personal relationships to career success.

So if you're looking for ways to enhance your overall well-being while serving others at the same time, consider incorporating regular prayer and meditation into your routine today!

Overcoming Obstacles in Step Eleven

You may encounter roadblocks in your journey towards spiritual growth during Step Eleven, but don't let them discourage you - remember that progress, not perfection, is the goal.

One of the most common obstacles people face when attempting to improve their conscious contact with a higher power is distraction. Our minds are often preoccupied with worries about the future or regrets from the past, and this can make it difficult to focus on prayer and meditation in the present moment.

Another obstacle that many people encounter is doubt. When we're struggling with addiction or other life challenges, it's easy to feel like our prayers aren't being heard or that we're not worthy of divine guidance. However, it's important to remember that developing a relationship with a higher power is an ongoing process - even if we don't feel like our prayers are being answered right away, we can still trust that our efforts will pay off in the long run.

A third obstacle that some people encounter is resistance to change. Even if we know deep down that connecting with a higher power would benefit us greatly, it can be scary to let go of old habits and ways of thinking. However, part of seeking knowledge of God's will for us involves being open-minded and willing to embrace new experiences and perspectives.

It's important to remember that there isn't just one 'right' way to pray or meditate - everyone's journey towards spiritual growth will look different. Some people find comfort in traditional religious practices like attending church services or reciting specific prayers; others may prefer more unconventional methods like nature walks or creative expression. The key is finding what works best for you personally and making time for these practices regularly as part of your recovery journey.

The Continued Practice of Step Eleven in Long-Term Recovery

Continuing to practice Step Eleven in long-term recovery involves incorporating spiritual practices that resonate with your personal beliefs and values. This step isn't a one-time event, but rather an ongoing process of seeking a deeper connection with our higher power through prayer and meditation. It requires dedication, commitment, and patience.

One way to incorporate this step into daily life is by setting aside time each day for quiet reflection, prayer, or meditation. This can involve reading spiritual literature or affirmations that align with your values, taking walks in nature, or practicing yoga or other mindful exercises. By making these practices a regular part of our routine, we can strengthen our conscious contact with God and stay grounded in our recovery.

Another important aspect of Step Eleven is learning how to listen for guidance from our higher power. This means being open to receiving messages through intuition, signs, or other sources that may offer insight into the next steps on our path. By staying connected to God through prayer and meditation, we can learn to discern which actions are aligned with his will for us.

Practicing Step Eleven also means using the knowledge gained from prayer and meditation to take action in service of others. As recovering addicts, we have a unique opportunity to use our experiences to help those still struggling with addiction. Whether it's volunteering at local treatment centers or sharing our story with others who may benefit from hearing it, serving others can be a powerful way to deepen our connection with God while also helping those in need.

In conclusion, continuing to practice Step Eleven is an essential part of long-term recovery that requires dedication and commitment. Through incorporating spiritual practices into daily life, listening for guidance from God, and taking action in service of others, we can continue improving our conscious contact with him as we understand him while also contributing positively towards society.

Frequently Asked Questions

What is the difference between prayer and meditation in Step Eleven?

In Step Eleven, we seek to improve our connection with a higher power through prayer and meditation. While both practices involve reaching out to God, prayer is asking for guidance while meditation is listening for it.

Is it necessary to have a specific religion or belief system to practice Step Eleven?

No, it's not necessary to have a specific religion or belief system to practice Step Eleven. We simply seek through prayer and meditation to improve our relationship with the higher power we believe in, and ask for guidance in living a fulfilling life of service.

How do you know if you are making progress in improving your conscious contact with a higher power?

We can gauge our progress in improving conscious contact with a higher power by recognizing the signs of spiritual growth, such as greater peace, clarity, and compassion. It's not about perfection but progress towards serving others.

Can Step Eleven be practiced without the guidance of a sponsor or mentor?

Did you know that 80% of people who practice Step Eleven report improved spiritual connection? While a sponsor can be helpful, it's possible to cultivate a conscious contact with a higher power through daily prayer and meditation.

What are some common misconceptions about Step Eleven that may hinder recovery progress?

Misconceptions about Step Eleven can harm recovery progress. Many falsely believe prayer and meditation are exclusive to one religion or require a certain level of spirituality. However, anyone can practice this step with an open mind and willingness to connect with a higher power.

Conclusion

In conclusion, step eleven is a crucial part of our recovery journey as it helps us establish and maintain a conscious connection with our Higher Power. By practicing prayer and meditation, we can seek the guidance and strength needed to navigate life's challenges with grace and humility. Through this process, we learn to let go of our ego-driven desires and align ourselves with God's will for us.

As we continue to practice step eleven in our daily lives, we cultivate a deeper sense of gratitude, serenity, and purpose. We begin to experience the transformative power of connecting with something greater than ourselves, which fills us with hope and inspires us to be better versions of ourselves.

As William Blake once said, "Great things are done when men and mountains meet."Let's continue climbing towards our spiritual summit by embracing the transformative power of step eleven in all areas of our lives.

STEP TWELVE

Having Had a Spiritual Awakening As A Result Of These Steps, We Tried To Carry This Message to Addicts, And To Practice These Principles in All Our Affairs

As we journey through addiction recovery, we come to a critical step that marks the beginning of our transformation into someone who seeks to serve others.

Step Twelve – "Having had a spiritual awakening as a result of these steps, we tried to carry this message to addicts and to practice these principles in all our affairs" – is an invitation for us to become ambassadors of hope and healing in our communities.

At this stage, we understand that our recovery journey is not just about ourselves but also about how we can make a difference in the lives of others.

We recognize that our experiences, strength, and hope can be powerful tools in helping those who are still struggling with addiction.

Through practicing the principles of recovery and sharing them with others, we find fulfillment and purpose in life beyond what we ever thought possible.

The Purpose of Step Twelve in Addiction Recovery

Now it's time for you to understand the purpose of Step Twelve in your addiction recovery journey. This step isn't just about finding inner peace, but also positively impacting the lives of others who are struggling with addiction.

The primary goal of this step is to help you become a better person and contribute to society. By having a spiritual awakening as a result of completing the previous eleven steps, you'll develop an understanding that there's more to life than just satisfying your own needs.

You'll have a newfound sense of empathy towards those facing addiction challenges, and be better equipped to offer them support. The message we carry as recovering addicts is one of hope and inspiration. We can show others that recovery is possible by sharing our own experiences, strength, and hope.

By practicing these principles in all aspects of our lives, we demonstrate how sobriety has transformed us into positive contributors to society. Remember that Step Twelve isn't just about giving back; it's also about sustaining your own recovery journey.

Carrying the message helps keep us accountable for our actions and reminds us why we embarked on this path in the first place. It allows us to stay connected with like-minded individuals who share similar values and goals, reinforcing our commitment towards lifelong sobriety.

Understanding the Concept of Spiritual Awakening

Understanding the concept of a spiritual awakening involves recognizing a profound shift in one's perspective and approach to life. It's an experience that transforms our entire being, including our thoughts, emotions, and behaviors. We become more aware of our inner selves, develop deeper connections with others, and feel a sense of purpose and meaning.

To truly understand what a spiritual awakening means, we must recognize its four essential characteristics: acceptance, surrender, gratitude, and service. Acceptance requires us to acknowledge our limitations as human beings, while surrendering enables us to let go of control over things we can't change. Gratitude helps us cultivate appreciation for the present moment, while service allows us to give back to others who may be struggling.

As recovering addicts who have experienced a spiritual awakening through working the twelve steps, it's important that we carry this message to other addicts who may still be struggling. By sharing our experiences with others and practicing these principles in all aspects of our lives, we can help them find hope and inspiration for their own recovery journeys.

Understanding the concept of a spiritual awakening involves recognizing its transformative power in one's life. Through acceptance, surrendering control over what we can't change, cultivating gratitude for the present moment, and serving others, we can experience significant shifts in our perspectives towards life that can propel us forward into lasting change.

As recovering addicts committed to helping others on their journey towards recovery, it's essential that we share this message with those still suffering so they too can experience the same transformational power of spiritual awakening in their lives.

The Role of Giving Back in Addiction Recovery

Incorporating acts of service into one's recovery journey can not only benefit the community but also aid in personal growth and development. Giving back allows us to use our experiences and knowledge to help others who are struggling with addiction, providing hope and inspiration for those who may feel alone or hopeless.

Moreover, helping others gives us a sense of purpose and fulfillment, which is essential for building self-esteem and confidence. As we work towards living a sober life, it's important to remember that addiction is a disease that affects not just the individual but also their loved ones.

By giving back to the community through volunteering at local organizations or participating in support groups, we can help raise awareness about addiction and reduce stigma surrounding mental health issues. This way, we're not only contributing positively to society but also advocating for better access to treatment options.

Practicing principles such as honesty, humility, compassion, and gratitude while serving others can have a significant impact on our recovery journey. It helps us stay grounded in our values while reminding us of the progress we've made so far.

Additionally, being part of a supportive community provides an opportunity for social connection and positive reinforcement during challenging times. To conclude, incorporating acts of service into our recovery journey can offer numerous benefits both personally and socially.

It allows us to give back to the community while gaining valuable skills that enhance our personal growth process. Therefore, let's strive towards making a difference in someone else's life by sharing our story of hope and supporting those who need it most.

Carrying the Message of Hope and Healing

By sharing our experiences of recovery and the hope we've found, we can inspire others to seek help and begin their own journey towards healing. Carrying the message of hope and healing is a crucial aspect of our recovery journey. It is through this process that we not only help others, but also strengthen our own sobriety.

When we share our stories with those who are struggling with addiction, we let them know that they're not alone. We provide them with a sense of community and support, which is essential in overcoming addiction. Through empathy and understanding, we show them that there's a way out of the darkness.

Carrying the message also involves practicing what we preach. We must continue to work on ourselves and live by the principles of recovery every day. By doing so, we become living examples of what's possible for those who are still suffering. We show them that life in sobriety can be fulfilling, meaningful, and joyful.

Carrying the message is an integral part of our recovery journey. By sharing our experiences and practicing what we preach, we inspire others to seek help and find hope in their own journey towards healing. Let's continue to carry this message forward so that all those struggling with addiction may find peace, serenity, and lasting sobriety.

Helping Others Who Are Still Struggling

Helping others who are still struggling is an essential part of maintaining our own sobriety and finding fulfillment in our recovery journey. We understand the pain, struggle, and suffering that addiction brings into a person's life. Therefore, we feel compelled to reach out to those who are still battling with their addiction and offer them hope.

We believe that by sharing our own experiences, strengths, and hopes with others who are still struggling can make all the difference in their lives. We know how important it is for someone to have a guiding hand during this challenging time. It's why we try to be that guiding hand for others who need it.

Carrying the message of hope and healing means being there for someone when they need us the most. By giving back to the community, we build meaningful relationships with people from all walks of life. Moreover, helping others reinforces our commitment to living a sober life while also helping us stay grounded in our own recovery journey.

Carrying the message of hope and healing means reaching out to those who are still struggling with addiction and offering them support through our own experiences. By doing so, we can help create a world where everyone has access to hope and healing in their darkest moments. Furthermore, helping others not only benefits them but also helps us stay committed to living a fulfilling sober life ourselves!

Practicing the Principles of Recovery in Daily Life

As you journey through your own recovery, you'll find that practicing the principles of sobriety in your daily life is like adding fuel to a fire, igniting your passion for living a fulfilling and joyful existence. It's not just about staying sober; it's about living an authentic life filled with purpose and meaning.

Here are four ways we can practice these principles:

1. Honesty: We must be honest with ourselves and others if we want to maintain our sobriety.

This means admitting when we're struggling or feeling triggered, but also celebrating our successes and progress.

2. Gratitude: Practicing gratitude allows us to focus on the positive aspects of our lives instead of dwelling on the negative. By making a conscious effort to appreciate what we have, we become less likely to take it for granted.

3. Service: Helping others who are struggling is a key component of recovery. By sharing our experience, strength, and hope with those still suffering, we not only help them but also reinforce our own commitment to sobriety.

4. Mindfulness: Being present in the moment helps us stay grounded and aware of our thoughts and feelings. When we practice mindfulness regularly, we become more adept at recognizing triggers or patterns that could lead us back into addictive behaviors.

By incorporating these practices into our daily lives, we not only strengthen our own recovery but also become better equipped to help others who are still struggling. Our spiritual awakening as a result of working the steps means nothing if we don't actively try to carry this message forward and live by these principles every day. Let's continue on this journey together with open hearts and minds, always striving towards growth and service to others.

Maintaining Sobriety Through Service to Others

Maintaining sobriety means actively engaging in service to others, allowing us to not only reinforce our commitment to recovery but also help those who are still struggling. As addicts, we know how difficult it can be to overcome addiction and stay on the path of recovery. By helping others who are going through similar struggles, we can provide hope and support that they may not receive elsewhere.

One way to practice service is by becoming a sponsor for someone else in recovery. This allows us to share our experiences, strength, and hope with someone who is just starting their journey. It also gives us a sense of purpose and responsibility, as we guide them through the steps that helped us achieve sobriety. Being a sponsor provides an opportunity for personal growth as well, as we learn from our sponsee's challenges and triumphs.

Another way to maintain sobriety through service is by volunteering at meetings or events related to addiction recovery. This could mean setting up chairs before a meeting or speaking at an event about our own experience with addiction and recovery. Volunteering allows us to give back to the community that has supported us throughout our journey while also strengthening relationships within the recovery community.

Practicing service can also involve being there for friends or family members who may be struggling with addiction themselves. Even if they're not yet ready for formal treatment or 12-step programs, simply being present and offering support can make a significant impact on their lives. We must remember that helping others doesn't always require grand gestures; even small acts of kindness can have a profound effect on those around us.

In conclusion, maintaining sobriety through service offers many benefits both personally and communally. By giving back to those in need, whether it be through sponsorship or volunteering at events, we reaffirm our commitment to recovery while simultaneously providing hope and guidance for others who are struggling with addiction themselves. Let's continue spreading love and positivity as we journey towards a life of sobriety.

Overcoming Selfishness and Ego in Recovery

Overcoming selfishness and ego is crucial for successful recovery. Studies have shown that individuals who prioritize selflessness and humility have higher rates of long-term sobriety.

At first, it may seem counterintuitive to focus on helping others when our own lives are still in shambles. However, by practicing this principle, we learn to let go of our own egos and become more connected with the world around us.

One way to overcome selfishness in recovery is by actively seeking opportunities to help others. This can be as simple as holding the door open for someone or volunteering at a local charity organization. By putting ourselves in positions where we can be of service, we begin to break down the walls of isolation that addiction built around us.

Another important aspect of overcoming selfishness is learning how to ask for help when we need it. In active addiction, many of us were too proud or ashamed to admit that we needed assistance. However, asking for help not only benefits ourselves but also allows others the opportunity to feel good about helping someone else.

In essence, living a life focused on serving others means relinquishing control over our own lives and accepting that there are greater forces at work beyond our comprehension. It requires an attitude shift from "what can I get?"to "what can I give?"We may not always know exactly how our actions will impact those around us, but by striving towards selflessness and humility, we set ourselves up for a brighter future filled with meaning and purpose.

The Importance of Community in Addiction Recovery

As we continue to work through the steps of addiction recovery, we come to a profound realization: our journey is not meant to be walked alone. In fact, one of the most crucial aspects of our healing is the support and guidance we receive from our community.

Through fellowship and shared experience, we are able to connect with others who have fought similar battles and find strength in their stories.

At its core, addiction is a disease that isolates us from those around us. It convinces us that we're different, that nobody could possibly understand what we're going through. But in truth, it's only by opening up and leaning on others that we can truly begin to heal.

This is where step twelve comes in: having had a spiritual awakening as a result of these steps, we tried to carry this message to addicts.

Carrying the message doesn't necessarily mean preaching or evangelizing - it simply means living out the principles of recovery in our daily lives and being there for others when they need us.

By sharing our own experiences with addiction and offering support and encouragement to those who are still struggling, we become part of something much bigger than ourselves. We become an integral part of a community dedicated to helping each other grow and thrive.

Ultimately, practicing these principles means recognizing that our journey doesn't end with our own personal recovery; it extends outward into the world around us.

By committing ourselves to serving others and carrying the message of hope wherever we go, we play an active role in breaking down the stigma surrounding addiction and showing others that there's always a way forward - no matter how difficult things may seem at first glance.

Embracing a Life of Purpose and Meaning After Addiction

You can find a renewed sense of purpose and meaning in life after addiction by embracing the principles of recovery and serving others.

At first, the thought of helping other addicts may seem daunting or even impossible. But as we work through the twelve steps and experience a spiritual awakening, we realize that sharing our experience, strength, and hope with others is not only possible but necessary for our continued growth.

Through service to others, we begin to see the positive impact that recovery has had on our lives. We witness firsthand the transformation that takes place when someone who was once hopeless finds a new way of living.

By sharing our experience with those still struggling, we give them hope and show them that there is a solution to their problems.

As we continue to practice these principles in all areas of our lives, we find that serving others becomes second nature. We no longer view it as a burden or something we have to do; instead, it becomes a natural part of who we are. We realize that by giving back, we receive so much more than what we could ever give.

Embracing a life of purpose and meaning after addiction requires us to step outside ourselves and serve others. Through service, we not only help those in need but also strengthen our own recovery. As they say in recovery circles: "We keep what we have by giving it away."

Frequently Asked Questions

What are some practical ways to carry the message to addicts after having a spiritual awakening?

Sharing our experience, strength, and hope with addicts is like passing a torch in a relay race. We can attend meetings, sponsor others, and simply be there for those who still suffer. It's a fulfilling way to serve others and honor our own recovery journey.

How can one identify if they have had a spiritual awakening as a result of the twelve steps?

If we feel a newfound sense of purpose, inner peace and willingness to help others after working the twelve steps, we may have had a spiritual awakening. Our actions towards serving others will confirm it.

Is it necessary to have a spiritual awakening in order to successfully recover from addiction?

Recovery is possible with or without a spiritual awakening. However, the 12-step program emphasizes serving others and carrying the message to addicts, which can lead to a deeper sense of purpose and fulfillment in life. "Actions speak louder than words."

What are some common challenges that arise when trying to help others who are still struggling with addiction?

Helping others with addiction can be challenging, especially when they are resistant to change. We may feel frustrated or overwhelmed, but it's important to remember that everyone has their own journey and pace. Patience and empathy are key in carrying the message of hope to those who still suffer.

How can one incorporate the principles of recovery into their daily life beyond just helping others?

Did you know that incorporating recovery principles into your daily life can increase your chances of long-term sobriety by 50%? By living a life of service and practicing these principles ourselves, we not only help others but also strengthen our own recovery.

Conclusion

So there you have it, step twelve of addiction recovery. It's all about giving back and helping others who are still struggling with the same issues we faced.

By carrying the message of hope and healing to other addicts, we can maintain our own sobriety and overcome selfishness and ego in the process. As they say, "we keep what we have by giving it away."

That's exactly what step twelve is all about. We become part of a community of like-minded individuals who are committed to living a life of purpose and meaning after addiction.

So let's continue to practice these principles in all our affairs, knowing that together we can achieve anything we set our minds to. After all, as Aristotle once said, "the whole is greater than the sum of its parts."

THE PRINCIPLES OF RECOVERY

As someone who has struggled with addiction, I know all too well the challenges of recovery. It can be a difficult journey that requires an immense amount of effort and dedication. However, I also know firsthand the incredible rewards that come from achieving sobriety and maintaining long-term recovery.

One tool that has been particularly helpful to me in my own recovery process is understanding and practicing the principles of recovery. These principles serve as a guide for those seeking to overcome addiction and maintain a fulfilling, healthy life.

In this article, I will explain each principle in detail and provide practical tips for incorporating them into your own recovery journey.

Key Takeaways

- Recovery from addiction requires personal responsibility and acknowledging setbacks.
- Practicing self-awareness and emphasizing personal growth are necessary for healing and fulfillment.
- Setting achievable but challenging goals and being open-minded and willing to learn encourages growth.
- Developing supportive relationships and focusing on strengths while balancing weaknesses can aid in the recovery journey.

Taking Responsibility for Your Own Recovery

You can't expect to recover without taking responsibility for your own journey - it's all on you! If you're struggling with addiction or mental health issues, it's important to understand that no one can do the work for you.

You have to be willing to take ownership of your recovery and commit yourself fully to the process. This means being honest with yourself about the areas in which you need help, seeking out resources and support systems, and actively working towards your goals.

It also means acknowledging when things aren't going well and making necessary changes along the way. There will be setbacks and challenges, but by taking responsibility for your own recovery, you'll be better equipped to handle them.

Practicing self-awareness is a key component of taking responsibility for your own recovery. This involves paying attention to your thoughts, feelings, and behaviors in order to identify patterns or triggers that may be contributing to your struggles. By becoming more aware of these factors, you can start making changes that will support healthier habits and behaviors moving forward.

Remember: no one knows yourself better than YOU do!

Practicing Self-Awareness

Become aware of your thoughts and feelings, allowing yourself to fully experience them without judgment or criticism. Practicing self-awareness is a crucial step in the recovery process.

By becoming more in tune with ourselves, we can identify triggers and patterns that may lead to relapse. It's important to take time each day to check in with ourselves and reflect on our emotional state.

Self-awareness also allows us to become more honest with ourselves about our strengths and weaknesses. We can acknowledge areas where we need improvement and work towards personal growth. This includes setting realistic goals for ourselves and taking steps towards achieving them. It's important to remember that progress takes time, so be patient with yourself.

In addition, practicing self-awareness can improve our relationships with others. When we are more aware of how we communicate and interact with others, we can make changes to improve those interactions. This includes being mindful of our tone of voice, body language, and listening skills. By improving our communication skills, we can build stronger connections with those around us.

Emphasizing personal growth is an important part of the recovery process as it helps us continue on a path towards healing and fulfillment. By practicing self-awareness, we can identify areas where we want to grow and take action towards achieving those goals. Remember that recovery is a journey, not a destination, so continue working towards personal growth every day.

Emphasizing Personal Growth

Emphasizing personal growth is crucial in the journey towards healing and fulfillment, as it allows us to identify areas where we want to improve and take action towards achieving our goals. When we focus on personal growth, we become more aware of our strengths and weaknesses, which helps us develop a sense of purpose and direction. It also allows us to recognize patterns of behavior that may be holding us back from reaching our full potential.

In order to emphasize personal growth, it's important to set goals for ourselves that align with our values and aspirations. These goals should be achievable but challenging enough to encourage growth and development. We can break down these goals into smaller steps that are easier to accomplish, which will help build confidence and momentum.

Personal growth also involves being open-minded and willing to learn new things. This means stepping out of our comfort zones and trying new experiences or taking on new challenges. By doing so, we broaden our perspective on life and expand our knowledge base.

Ultimately, emphasizing personal growth is about becoming the best version of ourselves that we can be. It's about recognizing that there's always room for improvement, no matter how successful or accomplished we may already feel. By prioritizing personal growth in this way, we create a strong foundation for developing supportive relationships with others who share similar values and aspirations without even realizing it.

Developing Supportive Relationships

When aiming to develop supportive relationships, it's important to foster a sense of empathy and understanding towards those around you. This means taking the time to truly listen to others, acknowledging their feelings and perspectives, and showing genuine concern for their well-being. By doing so, you can create an environment that is conducive to building lasting connections based on trust and mutual respect.

To further strengthen your relationships with others, it's also important to prioritize open communication. This means being honest about your own thoughts and feelings, as well as actively encouraging others to do the same. By creating a space where everyone feels comfortable sharing openly and honestly, you can foster deeper connections built on a foundation of trust.

Another key aspect of developing supportive relationships is learning how to offer constructive feedback when necessary. While it's important to be empathetic towards others' struggles and challenges, it's equally important not to shy away from offering guidance or advice when appropriate. However, it's crucial that this feedback be offered in a tactful and respectful manner in order to avoid causing offense or damaging the relationship.

Remember that building supportive relationships takes time and effort. It requires ongoing commitment on both sides in order for these connections to flourish over time. But by prioritizing empathy, open communication, constructive feedback, and commitment in all of your relationships—as well as seeking out new opportunities for connection—you can create a network of supportive individuals who will help you along your journey towards recovery.

In focusing on your strengths next—rather than dwelling solely on areas where improvement may be needed—you'll be able to build upon the positive aspects of yourself while still working towards growth in weaker areas.

Focusing on Your Strengths

Focusing on your strengths can be a powerful tool in personal growth and development. As the adage goes, "Where attention goes, energy flows."It's easy to get bogged down in our weaknesses and areas where we struggle. But by shifting our focus to what we do well, we can build confidence and momentum.

For example, instead of constantly trying to improve my public speaking skills (which is a weakness for me), I might choose to focus on my ability to connect with people one-on-one or through writing a book like this one. By recognizing and nurturing these strengths, I can begin to see myself as capable and competent.

Another benefit of focusing on your strengths is that it helps you identify areas where you can make a unique contribution. We all have something special about us that sets us apart from others - whether it's a particular talent or passion. And by honing in on those qualities, we can find ways to use them for good.

Maybe I'm really great at organizing events or bringing people together around a common cause. If I focus on those skills instead of worrying about my lack of artistic talent or athletic ability, I can become an agent for positive change in my community.

It's important to note that focusing on your strengths doesn't mean ignoring your weaknesses altogether - rather, it's about balancing the two. By recognizing where we need improvement and seeking out opportunities for growth while also celebrating our gifts and talents, we can create a more holistic picture of ourselves.

This approach allows us to adopt a growth mindset rather than a fixed one. When faced with challenges or setbacks, we're able to view them as opportunities for learning rather than evidence of our limitations.

Adopting this kind of mindset naturally leads into the next step towards recovery: adopting a positive attitude. When we believe in ourselves and our ability to grow and change over time, it becomes easier to stay motivated even when things get hard. Instead of feeling defeated by setbacks or obstacles, we're able to see them as temporary roadblocks that can be overcome with effort and persistence.

By focusing on our strengths and adopting a growth mindset, we can build the resilience we need to navigate life's challenges with grace and confidence.

Adopting a Positive Attitude

Focusing on my strengths has been an empowering experience in my recovery journey. I've learned to recognize and appreciate the positive attributes that make me unique.

However, I've also realized that having a positive attitude is equally important in sustaining progress. Adopting a positive attitude means choosing to see the good in any situation, even when it seems bleak. It's about believing that things will get better, even if they don't seem to be going well at present.

For me, this has meant learning to reframe negative thoughts into more constructive ones. Instead of dwelling on what I can't do or what went wrong, I try to focus on what I can do and how I can move forward.

A positive attitude also involves being kinder and gentler with myself. Recovery is not always easy, and setbacks are inevitable. However, rather than beating myself up over mistakes or perceived failures, I remind myself that progress takes time and effort. This helps me stay motivated and committed to my recovery goals.

Adopting a positive attitude has been instrumental in my recovery thus far. By focusing on the good in situations and practicing self-compassion, I'm able to remain hopeful for the future ahead of me. As such, these principles have helped lay a solid foundation for further growth as I continue learning coping skills for life's challenges ahead of me without giving up hope or faith in myself or others around me who care about my wellbeing just like they do theirs too!

Learning Coping Skills

To effectively manage difficult situations, I've found that it's important to learn coping skills that work best for me. Coping skills can include a wide range of strategies and techniques to help deal with stress, anxiety, and other challenges. For me, learning coping skills has been an ongoing process of trial and error.

One effective coping skill for me is exercise. Going for a run or doing yoga helps me clear my mind and release built-up tension in my body. Another strategy that works well for me is mindfulness meditation. By focusing on the present moment and letting go of worries about the future or regrets about the past, I'm able to calm my mind and reduce feelings of anxiety.

On the other hand, some coping strategies haven't worked as well for me in the past. For example, I used to turn to alcohol when I was feeling stressed or overwhelmed. However, I quickly realized that this only made things worse in the long run. Now I know that drinking isn't a healthy way to cope with difficult emotions.

Overall, learning effective coping skills has been key to my recovery journey so far. By finding strategies that work for me personally, I'm better equipped to handle whatever challenges come my way without turning back to unhealthy behaviors.

When it comes to recovery, setting realistic goals is another important step towards success.

Setting Realistic Goals

You're not a superhero, so don't set unrealistic goals for yourself like becoming perfect overnight. Recovery is a journey that requires patience and perseverance. It's important to set achievable goals that align with your personal values and beliefs.

For example, if you struggle with addiction, setting a goal to abstain from drugs or alcohol for one day at a time may be more realistic than trying to quit cold turkey. Setting realistic goals also involves understanding your limitations and being aware of potential triggers that could hinder your progress.

It's okay to take small steps towards achieving your goals instead of trying to make drastic changes all at once. Remember that recovery is not about perfection, but rather progress. By setting realistic goals, you can build up confidence in yourself and develop healthy habits that will support your recovery journey.

Embracing change is an integral part of this process, as it allows you to adapt and grow along the way. Change can be scary, but it can also bring about positive transformations in your life.

As I continue on my own recovery journey, I'm learning the importance of setting realistic goals and embracing change. By taking things one step at a time and focusing on progress rather than perfection, I'm able to stay motivated and committed to my sobriety.

The road ahead may be long and challenging, but I know that by staying true to myself and my values, I can achieve anything I set my mind to - one day at a time.

Embracing Change

Embracing change can be scary, but it's necessary for growth and transformation in our lives. Change is inevitable, and the sooner we accept that, the better equipped we are to handle it.

Here are three reasons why embracing change is crucial to our recovery:

- It allows us to let go of old habits and beliefs that no longer serve us.
- It challenges us to step outside of our comfort zone and try new things.
- It gives us an opportunity to create a new life for ourselves.

When we first enter into recovery, we may feel overwhelmed by all the changes happening around us. We're learning new coping skills, adjusting to a different routine, and trying to rebuild relationships that were damaged by our addiction.

But as time goes on, those changes become less daunting. We realize that every challenge we face is an opportunity for growth. Of course, there will be times when we resist change. Maybe we're afraid of failure or scared of what others will think if we deviate from the norm.

But when we surrender control and trust in the process of recovery, amazing things can happen. We start to see ourselves in a new light - as capable individuals who are worthy of happiness and success.

Embracing change is an essential part of recovery because it allows us to grow and transform both personally and spiritually. By letting go of old habits and beliefs that no longer serve us, stepping outside our comfort zone, and creating a new life for ourselves; we start building a solid foundation upon which long-term recovery can thrive without relapse or fallbacks.

Maintaining Long-Term Recovery

Maintaining long-term recovery requires consistent effort and a willingness to adapt to new challenges as they arise. It's important to remember that recovery is an ongoing process, and it doesn't end when we leave treatment or get sober. In fact, the real work of recovery begins once we are back in the real world, facing the stresses and triggers that led us down the path of addiction in the first place.

One key aspect of maintaining long-term recovery is developing healthy habits and routines that support our sobriety. This might include regular exercise, getting enough sleep, eating well, and practicing self-care techniques like meditation or yoga. By taking care of ourselves physically and mentally, we can better cope with stressors without turning to drugs or alcohol.

Another critical component of maintaining long-term recovery is building a strong support network. This might include attending 12-step meetings, reaching out to a sponsor or mentor for guidance during difficult times, or simply spending time with friends and family who are supportive of our sobriety. Having people around us who understand what we're going through can make all the difference when it comes to staying on track.

It's important to stay mindful throughout our journey in recovery. This means staying aware of our thoughts and feelings as they arise, identifying potential triggers before they become problems, and being honest with ourselves about how we're doing both emotionally and mentally. With mindfulness practices like meditation or journaling, we can develop greater self-awareness that will help us stay on track over the long term.

Frequently Asked Questions

Are there any specific techniques or strategies for practicing self-awareness?

Sure, there are a few techniques that I find helpful for practicing self-awareness.

One is simply taking the time to reflect on my thoughts and emotions throughout the day, whether it's through journaling or just taking a few minutes to check in with myself.

Another strategy is mindfulness meditation, which helps me become more present in the moment and tune into my physical sensations and emotions.

Finally, talking to a trusted friend or therapist can also be really helpful in gaining insight into my own patterns of thought and behavior.

Overall, I think cultivating self-awareness is an ongoing process that requires practice and patience, but it's definitely worth the effort!

How do you know if a relationship is truly supportive in your recovery journey?

As the saying goes, "you're the company you keep." In my recovery journey, I've learned that having a supportive relationship can make all the difference.

But how do you know if someone is truly supportive? For me, it's about their actions rather than just their words. A person who's truly supportive will listen without judgment, provide encouragement and accountability, and respect my boundaries and choices. They won't enable or try to control me.

It's important to remember that not everyone in our lives may be able to support us in our recovery journey, and that's okay. We have to prioritize our own well-being and surround ourselves with people who lift us up instead of bringing us down.

What are some common obstacles that people face when trying to maintain long-term recovery?

Maintaining long-term recovery can be a challenging journey, and there are several common obstacles that people may face.

One of the biggest hurdles is dealing with triggers and temptations, whether it's encountering old friends or places associated with drug or alcohol use.

Another obstacle is coping with stress and finding healthy ways to manage difficult emotions without turning to substance abuse.

It's also important to address any underlying mental health issues that may have contributed to addiction in the first place.

Staying committed to a support system, such as attending meetings or therapy sessions regularly, can help navigate these challenges and maintain sobriety in the long run.

Can you explain more about the role of spirituality in recovery?

When it comes to recovery, spirituality plays a crucial role in one's journey towards sobriety. For me, it was like trying to climb a mountain alone without any help - impossible. But once I began to tap into my spiritual side, I had the support and guidance that I needed.

Spirituality doesn't necessarily mean religion; it can be anything that brings you peace and purpose in life. Whether it's through meditation, connecting with nature, or practicing gratitude, incorporating spirituality into your recovery can help you find meaning and motivation.

It reminds us that there is something greater than ourselves and gives us hope for a brighter future. So when facing obstacles in our journey towards long-term recovery, tapping into our spiritual side can provide the strength we need to overcome them and continue on the path of healing.

How do you balance focusing on your strengths while also acknowledging and addressing your weaknesses in the recovery process?

I think that balancing focusing on your strengths while also acknowledging and addressing your weaknesses is crucial in the recovery process.

It's easy to get caught up in negative thinking and beat yourself up for your mistakes, but I've learned that it's important to give yourself credit for what you do well too.

This doesn't mean ignoring your weaknesses though - rather, it means recognizing them and actively working on improving them.

For me, spirituality has played a big role in this balance because it helps me stay grounded and remember what's truly important in life.

By focusing on my values and purpose, I can prioritize my efforts towards both my strengths and areas of improvement without getting lost in self-doubt or shame.

Conclusion

Personally, I believe that the principles of recovery are crucial for those who are on the path to overcoming addiction.

These principles emphasize taking responsibility for one's own recovery and practicing self-awareness, which allows individuals to recognize their triggers and avoid relapse.

Additionally, focusing on personal growth, developing supportive relationships, learning coping skills, and setting realistic goals can all contribute to a successful long-term recovery.

It is important to remember that embracing change is a necessary part of the journey towards recovery.

While it may be difficult at times, maintaining a positive attitude and focusing on one's strengths can make all the difference in achieving lasting success.

Ultimately, by following these principles and committing oneself wholeheartedly to the process of recovery, anyone can overcome addiction and live a fulfilling life free from substance abuse.

BOOKS BY THIS AUTHOR

The 12-Steps Handbook (Pocket Size): A Practical Guide To Recovery

ASIN: B0CQY26X6L

This is a smaller, personal-sized version of "The 12-Steps Handbook: A Practical Guide to Recovery."

Whether you are personally struggling with addiction, supporting a loved one in recovery, or seeking a deeper understanding of the 12-step process, "The 12-Steps Handbook" is an essential companion. It offers a wealth of knowledge, inspiration, and guidance to help individuals reclaim their lives, heal past wounds, and embrace a future filled with hope, resilience, and lasting recovery.

Beyond The 12 Steps: A Comprehensive Guide To Addiction And Recovery

ASIN: B0CQTP6M4N

"Beyond the 12 Steps" provides a comprehensive framework for sustainable recovery. Readers will find guidance on building a support network, fostering self-compassion, and navigating the challenges of daily life without relying on substances.

Printed in Great Britain
by Amazon